CONSTANT FELLOWSHIP

CONSTANT FELLOWSHIP

A Handbook On Scripture Meditation

MIRIAM K. CHAMPLIN

TATE PUBLISHING & Enterprises

Published by Tate Publishing & Enterprises, LLC
127 E. Trade Center Terrace | Mustang, Oklahoma 73064 USA
1.888.361.9473 | www.tatepublishing.com

Tate Publishing is committed to excellence in the publishing industry. The company reflects the philosophy established by the founders, based on Psalm 68:11,
"The Lord gave the word and great was the company of those who published it."

Book design copyright © 2011 by Tate Publishing, LLC. All rights reserved.
Cover design by Sarah Kirchen
Interior design by Chelsea Womble

Published in the United States of America

ISBN: 978-1-61346-145-7
1. Religion, Biblical Meditations, General
2. Religion, Christian Life, Personal Growth
11.08.18

DEDICATION

In gratitude to the Spirit of grace and truth, who, from the beginning, has been my Chief Teacher.

ACKNOWLEDGMENTS

Special thanks to Dr. Layton Talbert, an esteemed mentor and friend, whose counsel has been a good and instrumental gift from the Father, and to my brother Matthew Champlin, whose friendship and wisdom have graced both my life and the process of writing this book. Amparo Pennington faithfully prayed for me and for the book through every step of the process, while Maria Case repeatedly read the manuscript and offered invaluable feedback. To both of these dear friends, among many unmentioned others, I am grateful.

PREFACE TO THE READER:

Knowing God is the most important thing in life. The very idea that God can be known originates with God Himself and comes to us as a gift from Him. God is God. He is transcendent. It is inconceivable that people like us could know Him. But God has determined to make Himself known to the people He created, and particularly to the people He has redeemed. God has purposed to *be known by* His people. When a child of God sees God for who He is, that child's response will be delight. To see God is to love Him.

So how do we learn to see God? How do you see that which is invisible? Can unseen things be as real and impacting as the daily life that surrounds us? Consider this: Has someone ever described something or someone to you, and based on their description, you "saw" that thing/person in your mind's eye? I think most of us have experienced that—a mental "seeing" of something, or even someone, that we have never seen before. This familiar experience helps answer the question of how we can see God. God designed a means through which His people can learn to see Him for who He really is and find their delight in Him supremely. Scripture calls this God-given means "meditation." We learn to see God with the eye of faith as we take what

He tells us about Himself and meditate on it. The more we ponder truth (or lies), especially truth (or lies) about God, the more real it becomes to us. We start seeing and knowing who God is and that impacts our lives. In the words of 2 Corinthians 3:18, we "beholding...are... being transformed..."

Stop and think about it: God never commands you to read your Bible every day. Most western Christians tend to believe that reading the Bible every day is one of the most basic fundamentals of Christian growth; but the Bible never says that. Why? Because, for the vast majority of believers throughout history, that has been an impossibility. Most of them did not have a written copy of God's Word available to them, and many of them could not read. But isn't spiritual growth rooted in hearing, believing, and obeying the Word of God? Well, yes. In fact, although the Bible does not command the believer to read Scripture on a prescribed schedule, it clearly emphasizes the primacy of the Word by repeatedly giving another command—one that is much more far-reaching and difficult to obey. The Bible tells you to meditate day and night. Day and night—continuously. This is a command that reaches the level of the heart. For you to obey this, the Word has to be in you. You have to want this and be committed to it. If obedience to this command was merely a matter of reading a portion of Scripture each day, you could perform the reading as a ritual, but since the command is to meditate day and night, no perfunctory treatment will suffice. You have to devote your heart and soul to obey. Once again, God reaches beyond the external and targets the heart.

Think of it carefully;
Study it prayerfully,
Deep in your heart let its oracles dwell;
Ponder its mystery,
Slight not its history;
For none ever loved it too fondly or well.

—Unknown

We all live life all day, every day—daily life is real to us. But most of us do not fellowship with God all day every day or even meditate on God regularly (if at all). Is it any wonder that God seems less real to us than the rest of life? Is it surprising that our view of God fluctuates depending on our circumstances at any given moment, rather than our view of our circumstances resting firmly on the truth about God and the reliability of His promises?

Psalm 1 paints a beautiful picture of a stable, healthy, productive tree growing beside a river—a tree that prospers even in drought. The analogy is simple: the prosperous, satisfied, stable person is one who is rooted in the Word of God—the Truth that God has revealed. This person engages in continual meditation on the truth; he finds his delight in the Word of God, and his life is solid and robust—connected, through meditation, with what is real and lasting. Meditation is essential to knowing God and sustaining spiritual life and health (Joshua 1:8; James 1:22–25).

So what is meditation, and how does one cultivate this lofty-sounding habit "day and night"? Meditation has multiple facets, but probably two major categories. First, meditation is an intentional focusing of your mind and heart on God and His Word. It is taking up individual truths about God as revealed in His Word and turning those truths over in your mind, purposefully, prayerfully, repeatedly. It is studying the Word deeply to master and be mastered by its teaching. This involves a conscious commitment of time and energy. It takes work, discipline, and carefulness. By the grace of God, you must choose to do this. This is the type of meditation that we see modeled in the lives of many of the Old Testament saints: Daniel and his regular patterns of prayer and reading of the prophets; David and his psalms flowing from his reflections on the character and ways of God; Enoch and his walk with God.

The second kind of meditation grows out of the first. This meditation is like the righteous counterpart of worrying. When you are worried about something, your mind goes back to that issue as often as it can. The moment that you are not completely occupied by another task or demand, your mind returns to its worry and stays there until pulled away by some other force. Similarly, the second type of meditation occurs when your mind goes back to think on God, again and again, as often as it gets opportunity, all day long. In computer terminology, meditation is when your mind's screensaver, its default mode, is set on Biblical truth, and all day long, whenever there is a break in the day's activity or a mindless task to be done, up comes the screensaver—the portraits of God and His ways that you, in times of intentional meditation, have stored up in your mind's eye. This is the "day and night" concept described in Scripture. It ties in with Paul's instructions on continual prayer (1 Thess. 5:17), thinking on praiseworthy things (Phil. 4:8), and setting the affections on eternal things (Col. 3:1). This is the mindset out of which Psalm 19 and Psalm 119 were written.

Knowing God is the most important thing in life; in fact, it is the only thing worth giving your life to. Knowing God and making Him known constitutes the highest privilege and joy in human experience. If that sounds like an overstatement to you, I would suggest that you do not really know God…yet. The purpose of this handbook, then, is to encourage you to know God. May it help you to begin cultivating the discipline of meditation—taking what God has revealed about Himself and examining it; scrutinizing the character of God, seeing Him for who He is, gazing on His glory, and worshipping Him. It pleases and glorifies God to be studied and admired by His children. He has said, "Seek My face" (Psalm 27:8). May this little book help enable you to respond to Him, "Your face, Lord, do I seek" (esv), and aid you in your pursuit of the "surpassing worth of knowing Christ Jesus" (Phil. 3:8, esv).

INTRODUCTION AND INSTRUCTIONS

HOW TO USE THIS HANDBOOK
IN THE MOST HELPFUL WAY.

I hope you read the preface. If you did not, please go back and read it. The preface gives the big picture and goal of this book, and without the goal (knowing God) in mind, most of this book becomes another meaningless religious exercise. The preface lays the foundation for the book, and this introduction will, I hope, give you practical tools that will enable you to get the maximum amount of profit from the book. Here is a list of basic suggestions:

1. Read this book as a companion to your Bible, not the other way around. Nothing can or should substitute for time in the Word and, when you do turn to read this, keep your Bible out and take time to look up the references and cross-references. This book is designed to help you get into the Word but, unless you are pro-active in embracing the proffered help, you will walk away with minimal benefit.

2. Always have a pen and paper on hand. You may not use them every time, but you will find your-self using them more and more as you go on.

3. Do not read too much in one sitting. The read-ings are of varying lengths, and some of the

longer ones are divided into several parts. You may wish to read more than one at a time, but in meditation, it is quality, not quantity, that you are striving for. It is far better to allow one truth to sink into your soul thoroughly and resonate there than to rush through exposure to multiple truths and be temporarily dazzled but walk away unchanged.

4. Take your time. Even if you do not have more than a few minutes to read, spend your few minutes deliberately. If you rush through because you feel like you are under time pressure, you are not really meditating and absorbing. You can waste your precious minutes by being frazzled, or you can invest them by being intentional and deliberate.

5. Read prayerfully. Ask the Spirit to teach you how to appropriate the principles and patterns outlined in this book and how to apply them in your own relationship with Him. Ask Him to be your Teacher. Ask Him to teach you to meditate, to teach you to know Him. Ask Him to give you discernment, wisdom, and insight in pursuing Him. Remember, God is a God who makes Himself known. He is eager for you to know Him, and He will help you as you diligently seek Him (Prov. 8:17—Start now! Look it up!).

6. Do not develop a "checklist mentality." Meditation is not just one more spiritual exercise or routine to walk through. This book is not meant to become a mindless routine or drudgery any more than meditation should be a mere routine exercise. There is no prescribed time frame you need to adhere to, nor do you need to read it all in order. There is an overall

pattern to the readings, but it is not at all necessary for you to read it straight through. Feel free to move around.

7. Regarding the reader notes at the bottom of many of the pages: that is the "handbook" part of this handbook. The notes will give you personal comment and history, insights and methods, and suggestions for practical implementation. They are not intended as homework! Do not feel bound to follow the suggestions slavishly! They are not prescriptive. They are simply there so that, when you find yourself asking, "Where do I even start?" you have some suggestions of good places to begin. They are intended to be launching points if, and when, you find yourself in need of a launching point.

There are many forms of meditation, and you can meditate on any subject, but, for the purposes of this book, we will use "meditation" to refer to the Scriptural meaning of meditation which is focused primarily on the person and work of the Godhead. So, when you see the word "meditation," be thinking about intentionally focusing on God. This handbook contains three basic patterns of meditation:

1. Stockpiling names or attributes of God: i.e. recalling and recording a multitude of truths about God all at once in order to renew your mind, refresh your soul, and rejoice your heart in the greatness and glory of God's manifold perfections.

2. Individual investigations. Go through a book, a testament, or the whole of Scripture and trace out a name or an attribute of God for indi-

vidual consideration and admiration. This is a profitable means of plumbing the deep riches of God's unfathomable character and ways.

3. Prayers. Pray in light of who God is, whether in praise, in confession, in commitment, or in intercession.

These three basic patterns intertwine throughout the book. The length of the readings will vary. Sometimes it will simply be a single verse; other times, it will be several pages long. Read carefully, thoughtfully, and prayerfully. Do not allow yourself to rush through; instead, be intentional about letting truth about the God of heaven sink into your heart. Of all the topics for thought and discussion in the entire universe, God is the most worthy, the most sobering, and the most inexhaustible. So come and meditate on Him. Come and know God.

TABLE OF CONTENTS

1. A MORNING PRAYER

Blessed Redeemer, for Your own good pleasure, You created the world and all that is in it, and yet the crowning work of creation—man—consistently refuses to live for Your good pleasure and to the praise of Your glory. Help me not to follow the example of the first Adam today, but rather of the second Adam. The second Adam delighted to do Your will, O Father—He did what pleased You. Make me like Him. I love Him. He is my Lord and my God, my Redeemer and my King. I gladly surrender the throne of my heart to Him. I take up the armor that He gives and look to Him expectantly for strength to be His good soldier today.

2. SELECTED SCRIPTURES ON CHRIST

For Christ is the End of the law for righteousness to every one that believes. (Rom. 10:4)

For no other foundation can anyone lay than that is laid, which is Jesus Christ. (1 Cor. 3:11)

And you are Christ's; and Christ is God's. (1 Cor. 3:23)

…the power of our Lord Jesus Christ. (1 Cor. 5:4)

…Christ our Passover was sacrificed for us. (1 Cor. 5:7)

One of the simplest and sweetest forms of meditation is spending some time pulling together verses or phrases pertaining to a particular member of the Trinity or to a certain attribute of God. You can do this in your head, drawing on the truths and passages that you have accumulated in your heart and mind, or you can enlist the help of a concordance, a Bible software program, or a study Bible. You can do this with verses, with names of God, or with attributes of God. The next several meditations will provide some examples of this.

Miriam K. Champlin

3. NAMES OF CHRIST

Christ: the Power of God and the Wisdom of God.
Christ: the Prince of life.
Christ: the Lord of glory.
Christ: the Savior.
Christ: the King.
Christ: the Righteous.
Christ: my Lord.

4. MY JESUS

Jesus.
Jesus: my Lord.
Jesus: my Teacher.
Jesus: my Beloved.
Jesus: my only Hope.
Jesus.
Jesus: my Joy.
Jesus: my King.
Jesus: my Brother.
Jesus: my Advocate.
Jesus.
Jesus: my Master.
Jesus: my Righteousness.
Jesus: my Redeemer of my soul.
Jesus: my Great, Merciful, and Faithful High Priest.
Jesus.
Jesus: Friend.
Jesus: Lord.
Jesus: Life.
Jesus: All.
Jesus.

Miriam K. Champlin

After you have finished working through a meditation like this, if the truths are really sinking into your soul, your heart will be full of worship in response to what God has been teaching you about Himself. Let your worship overflow in song or in a prayer of thanksgiving to God. Hymns like "Be Thou my Vision," "Come, Thou Fount," "O Worship the King," and many, many others wed jubilant adoration with contemplative prayer for ever-increasing closeness to Him.

5. YOUR NAME

Savior.
Lamb.
Atonement.
Propitiation.
Redeemer.

What could we say of You that would accurately convey Your preciousness? How can we most fully see, savor, and show forth Your worth? You are so glorious. It is fitting for You to receive honor, glory, power, blessing, riches, wisdom, and strength (Revelation 4:11; 5:12). From You and through You and to You are all things (Romans 11:36). Your Name is Jesus, and You are the Lord.

Miriam K. Champlin

6. A MORNING PRAYER

My dearest Lord, Your love is overwhelming. You are so kind. "When morning gilds the skies, my heart, awaking, cries, 'May Jesus Christ be praised!' Alike at work or prayer, to Jesus I repair: May Jesus Christ be praised."[1] You are worthy of honor, glory, and blessing. You have created all things, and for Your pleasure they are and were created. You have created, and You have redeemed! "How marvelous! How wonderful! And my song shall ever be: How marvelous! How wonderful is my Savior's love to me!" Your love is compelling, because we reckon that if One died for all, then those who were given life by His death should not live in disregard of this One, but should, rather, live for the One who died for them and rose again. And this is only reasonable. How could redeemed ones do otherwise? Yet this is not mere duty; it is delight, because the One who loved and gave Himself now lives to intercede. To know Him and His Father is Life Eternal. Moreover, He is pleased to call out disciples and worshippers to be with Him where He is, and nothing in life is better than His presence. It is worth anything that a person could possibly "give up," endure, etc., to be with Him. There is no one like Him!

My own Lord, let me live with You today, to worship and serve You as it is fitting. You are worthy, and my soul yearns to please You. I love You and will obey You today. I take up the armor and go forth in Your Name. "Jesus, Thy blood and righteousness my beauty are, my glorious dress ..." Thank You.

7A. A MEDITATION ON THE BLOOD OF CHRIST

…our Lord Jesus Christ who gave Himself for our sins …(Gal. 1:4b-5a)

…the Son of God who loved me and gave Himself for me. (Gal. 2:20)

…Him that loved us and washed us from our sins in His own blood …(Rev. 1:5)

…Christ died for the ungodly. (Rom. 5:6)

…My blood of the new covenant which is shed for many for the remission of sins. (Matt. 26:28)

…the new covenant in My blood which is shed for you. (Luke 22:20)

…the church of God, which He purchased with His own blood. (Acts 20:28)

…having now been justified by His blood …(Rom. 5:9)

…in Him we have redemption through His blood, the forgiveness of sins, according to the riches of His grace …(Eph. 1:7)

…brought near by the blood of Christ. (Eph. 2:13)

…having made peace through the blood of His cross. (Col. 1:20)

...how much more shall the blood of Christ...
cleanse your conscience from dead works to serve
the living God. (Heb. 9:14)

...boldness to enter into the Holiest by the blood
of Jesus...(Heb. 10:19)

...that He might sanctify the people with His own
blood, suffered outside the gate. (Heb. 13:12)

...redeemed...with the precious blood of Christ
as of a lamb without blemish and without spot. (1
Pet. 1:18–19)

...the blood of Jesus Christ His Son cleanses us
from all sin. (1 John 1:9)

...You were slain and have redeemed us to God
by Your blood out of every tribe and tongue and
people and nation...(Rev. 5:9)

...robes...made white in the blood of the Lamb...
(Rev. 7:14)

And He was clothed with a robe dipped in blood,
and His name is called the Word of God. (Rev.
19:13)

So worship Him. Kneel before Him. Be brought near
to God by Him. Be united with Him. He died so that
you could live *in Him*. Give Him the obedience He
deserves. Satisfy Him by being satisfied with Him.
Give Him thanks. Adore Him. Praise Him. Crown
Him. Live life from Him, through Him, and to Him.
Let nothing in your life be too precious for Him, but
rather give all to Him who loved you and gave Himself
for you. He is worthy.

As stated earlier, this type of meditation can be developed quite simply using a concordance, or, faster yet, a Bible program on your computer. Select a couple of key words, search them, and then sort through the relevant verses and arrange them according to your specific focus. Take time to look up some or all of the verses in their contexts or perhaps in different versions. This will help you key into various facets of the verses and gain a richer under-standing of the concept. Looking up the verses will also keep you aware of the larger context in which each verse occurs and thus help prevent you from using a verse in a way that is inconsistent with the intent of the passage.

7B. WHY DID GOD SAVE US?

"…because of His great love with which He loved us…" (Eph. 2:4).

Tip: Choose a summary verse. After I have walked through a meditation such as the previous one, where I focused on one specific facet of God's character, Christ's work, etc., I find that picking out a single verse that concisely encapsulates the entire concept and keeping that verse in the forefront of my mind throughout the following day(s) really cements the truth in my heart. The verse could be one that, like Ephesians 2:4, gives the reason underlying the revelation of the truth considered, or it could just be one that ties most of your thoughts together effectively and beautifully—in a way that will cause your heart to sing praise to God whenever that verse comes to mind throughout the day.

8. JESUS THE SAVIOR

Savior: "…call His name Jesus, for He will save His people from their sins." (Matt. 1:21)

Think of the human state apart from Christ. Think of the sin that happens throughout your life. Think of all the sin that happens throughout even one day. Think of all the selfish reactions. Think of all the critical judgments of others. Think of the stench of your own pride and self-righteousness. Consider all your vain imaginations. Consider your impure thoughts. Ponder the foolish words, the prayerless conversations, the hasty answers. Face the self-idolization. Think of your spiritual adultery against your Creator—He who has the right to all of you. Take time to examine your depravity. You are dead in trespasses and sins. You have no life. You are bound for eternal damnation. You are hopeless, helpless, alienated, separated from God. You are wicked. You are unholy. You do not know God, and you cannot know God.

You need a savior. Without a savior, you are condemned.

You must know this. You must feel the weight of your sin and hopelessness. You must become desperate. You must long for a savior. You must cry to God.

God sees and knows you. He is your Maker. He is your Judge. He is the God of Eternal Glory. He has perfect right to do with you whatever He deems right. You stand guilty before Him and His righteous Word.

But God loves you. He loves you. His heartbeat is holy mercy, and He has determined from before the foundation of the world to pursue a relationship with you. He has chosen to bring Himself glory by sending a Savior to restore the shattered fellowship.

God sent a Savior. His Name is Jesus, and He saves His people from their sins.

There is no one else like Him. Truly, He is a wonderful Savior.

Treasure Him.
Admire Him.
Adore Him.
Worship Him.
Know Him.
Rejoice in Him.
Fear Him.
Glorify Him.
Love Him.
Look to Him and be saved.

Notice that the focus of this meditation is a bit more applied—that is, it considers how the fact that Jesus is the Savior affects me personally. It examines my need and my hopelessness, how Jesus changed that for me, and how I ought to respond to Him. It is good to have a balance between prayer and meditations that focus primarily on God Himself (doxological) and prayer and meditations that focus on wedding the truth about God to the truth about myself and exploring how the truth about God changes me and my daily life (orthopraxical).

9. A PRAYER OF CONFESSION

O my God, merciful and gracious, longsuffering and abounding in love, God of goodness and Giver of all good, it is true that I "have no good apart from you" (Ps. 16:2, ESV). These past several days I have been sleeping in and not spending much time with You. It is horrible. I have been starving my inner man and putting off the Light of my eyes, the Desire of my heart, the Joy of my countenance, the Life of my life. How is it that I become skewed with such abominable swiftness? How is it that I refuse to drink from the fountain that daily sustains me and that I would claim to love and need? Ah, I am grieved to have grieved You like this. I mourn that I have so lightly and sinfully treated You. Please, forgive me for Jesus' sake, because He exhausted the wrath that should fall on me for lightly handling the privilege and the command to draw near. Thank You for a Substitute, the sin-bearing Lamb slain for me. Lord, if You marked iniquity, no one could stand. Thank You for forgiveness. Truly, Your mercy causes me to fear Your Name (Ps. 130). Thank You for making me a recipient of mercy—so often, so completely, so patiently. Now through the washing of water by the Word, please cleanse my heart, renew my mind, and bow my soul in worship and thanksgiving. Thank You for a Savior, my Savior Jesus. Please, Lord, be Lord of me in every regard. O reflect Yourself in me! Cause me to so reflect on You that You are seen and known and heard through me. Above all, teach me to worship You. I need Your grace, and I look for Your mercy, and I hope in Your strength and salvation. Thank You for being my God.

The truth about Christ as your Savior affects how you respond when you sin and lose your fellowship with God. Use the truths that you have stored up in your heart and mind through meditation to lead you back to the right perspective, and then humbly and openly confess your sin, embrace the forgiveness He promises, and continue walking in the light (1 John 1).

10. MY ADVOCATE

Christ's word to Peter: "But I have prayed for you..."
(Luke 22:32)

> "He ever lives above for me to intercede
> His all-redeeming love His precious blood to plead.
> His blood atoned for all our race,
> His blood atoned for all our race,
> And sprinkles now the throne of grace."

> "The Father hears Him pray: His dear Anointed One.
> He cannot turn away the presence of His Son.
> His Spirit answers to the blood;
> His Spirit answers to the blood;
> And tells me I am born of God."[2]

Tip: Sing. Or at least feel free to use the words of songs that you know and love to voice your praises and prayers. God has given many of His children the ability to write lyrics and combine them with melodies with a result that is powerful and easy to remember. Make use of this good gift from God!

11. UNLIMITED GOOD

O limitless the love of Christ,
And limitless His grace;
His mercy flows afresh each day
To those who seek His face.

We who know You have found that this is true. You have poured out Your love in our hearts through the Holy Spirit, and we sing and rejoice because of Your abundant mercy. You are so good to us, Your children. How excellent is Your lovingkindness, O God! We do well to put our trust under the shadow of Your wings. We do well to rest in the possession of Christ and of every good thing for all eternity, because of Christ and in Christ.

12. HIS WORK OF REDEMPTION

Redeemed. This is a glorious truth! Delivered! Saved! Rescued! And You have done it. Although I lived in the pit of the earth—although I had no hope for salvation—although my life was one of rebellion and strife against You—although in me there was nothing good—although I was guilty, vile, and helpless, You are love, and You have loved me and made me Your own. You have fitted me to receive a portion of the lot of the inheritance of the saints in light (Ephesians 1; Colossians 1). You have brought me back from my allegiance to Satan, self, sin, and death, and have paid the debt of my sin to the Father. Christ Jesus, You bore my iniquity in Your own body on the tree, and me, even me—dead in my sins—You brought to life. You are the Redeemer, and I am Your redeemed one. You are the Savior, and I am Your delivered one. I glory in You, in knowing You, in Your cross. May it never be that I should boast in anything except these things. All other boasting is vain. It is Christ and Christ alone in whom I may boast.

This meditation and the next two are quite short and simple. That is on purpose. Let me remind you and encourage you to remind yourself that meditation is not as complex and daunting as we often imagine it to be. God commands us to meditate day and night, which means that meditation has to have practical implications and applications for every single child of God. Meditation is a step of obedience that is accessible to every believer. Do not let yourself be overwhelmed by how involved the task could be. Start with who you are and what you already know and grow from there. You do not have to—in fact, you cannot—turn into David the shepherd-king-psalmist overnight.

13. HIS NAMES

Faithful Servant, God with us, Son of Man, the Lord.
  Jesus, my Lord, my God, my Life.
  The Anointed One, the Lamb, the Redeemer.

14. HIS PERSON

Precious, marvelous Savior, accept the freewill offerings of my mouth. I praise You. I consider Your attributes: faithfulness, steadfastness, truth. I ponder Your graces: mercy, gentleness, justice, wisdom. I meditate on Your glories: majesty, strength, righteousness, riches, honor, dominion, infinity. I bless You: Holy One, Lamb, Jesus, Shepherd, Fountain of Life. Yes, I praise You.

Miriam K. Champlin

15. A MORNING PRAYER

Sun of my soul, rise in full strength and bring all Your light and energizing power to bear on my life today. Leave no corner shrouded in darkness, no weakness unflooded with Your strength. Let none of my perspectives settle down and dictate my day, but rather come and teach me to see as You see, to think as You think, to serve as You serve, to love based on Your love, to be like You, to represent You accurately and attractively. I do love You, and I make these requests known to You, as I put on the armor and head out to the day that You have put in front of me. Show Yourself strong, Worthy Champion. I adore You.

16. MEDITATIONS ON THE WONDERFULNESS OF CHRIST

"And His Name will be called Wonderful..." (Isa. 9:6).

Wonderful in strength. Yes, O Lord, doing mighty deeds to Your own glory. Strong to save and to rescue from death. Omnipotent. The Son of God with power. Mighty to perform the good pleasure of Your own perfect will. Our God is in the heavens; He has done whatever He has pleased. Wonderful in strength.

Wonderful in holiness. Matchlessly beautiful in Your set-apartness. Marvelous in Your superior separateness from all that You have made by the Word of Your power. You relate to every grace and every good thing (all of which come from You) in a unique way. There is no one who can touch Your complete otherness. Wonderful in holiness.

Wonderful in love. Gracious Savior who loved Your own even to the end. Unfathomable, steadfast love. Sacrificial, unconditional love. Love that will not let go. Incomprehensible love that takes no pleasure even in the death of the wicked. Redemptive, righteous, eternal love. Wonderful in love.

Wonderful in wisdom. Indeed, all the treasures of wisdom and knowledge are hidden in You. As the psalmist would say, Your knowledge is too wonderful for me; it is high; I cannot attain it (Ps. 139:6). You weigh out the measures of the universe by Your wisdom, and because You are strong in power, not one of them fails. Your wisdom and Your sovereignty go hand in hand in the lives of Your children. We may surely trust You, because You are wonderful in wisdom.

Wonderful in goodness. Your Word calls, "Oh, taste and see that the LORD is good" (Ps. 34:8). Yes, You are good. Full of goodness. Rich in goodness. You are good to the just and the unjust; You send Your rain and Your sunshine on the righteous and the unrighteous. Your goodness is not capricious and driven by whim. Your goodness is sure and steadfast, sweet and settled. Wonderful in goodness.

Wonderful in righteousness. You will always do what is right. There is no spot or blemish in You, nor is there any of Your work that is not done in judgment and truth. Your righteousness is very high, O God. Brilliant righteousness. Pure righteousness. Enduring righteousness. Wonderful in righteousness.

Wonderful in truth. Are not Your eyes on the truth, O LORD? You love truth. You desire truth in the inward parts. Truth is beautiful in Your sight, and high is the value that You have set on it. As for Yourself, You are true. There is no falsehood, no darkness, in You at all. You are the Truth. You do truth. Pure truth. You are wonderful in truth.

Wonderful in grace. You are the God of all grace. All Your dealings are saturated with divine grace. We cannot comprehend Your grace. Your grace is transcendent, yet so near. The nearness of Your grace, because

You are a God at hand, is a comfort and strength. Your children need grace so desperately, and indeed, we find You to be wonderful in grace.

Wonderful in purity. Pure God, without iniquity, without spot, without weakness, without lack. You are alone in Your absolute purity. There is none who can compare with You. To see You in Your radiant, blinding purity is something that no man can do and live. But in heaven, You will make us pure, and we will see Your face and rejoice in You. Wonderful in purity.

Isaiah 9:6 is a familiar verse, and it is often the well-known verses that we skip over the most quickly or find the most difficult to meditate on. Their familiarity makes us think that we already know what they are talking about and that we do not need to ponder them much. As I read Isaiah 9:6 one morning, the Lord was gracious enough to make me pause to stop and ask, "If Christ will be called 'Wonderful,' what does that wonderfulness look like? What about Christ is wonderful?" And as I prayed and asked for insight and understanding to know Christ better, these are some of the thoughts that the Spirit brought to mind for me to consider and delight in.

Miriam K. Champlin

17. PSALM 25

O LORD, I come before You in prayer.
　　My God, I trust in You.
　　　　Please do not let me be humiliated;
　　　　Do not let my enemies triumphantly rejoice over me!
　　Certainly none who rely on You will be humiliated.
　　　　Those who deal in treachery will be thwarted and humiliated.
Make me understand Your ways, O LORD!
Teach me Your paths!
Guide me into Your truth and teach me.
　　　　For You are the God who delivers me;
　　　　on You I rely all day long.
Remember Your compassionate and faithful deeds, O Lord,
　　　　for You have always acted in this manner.
Do not hold against me the sins of my youth or my rebellious acts!
　　　　Because You are faithful to me, extend to me Your favor, O LORD!
The LORD is both kind and fair;
　　　　that is why He teaches sinners the right way to live.
　　　　　　May He show the humble what is right!
　　　　　　May He teach the humble his way!
The LORD always proves faithful and reliable to those who follow the demands of His covenant.
For the sake of Your reputation, O LORD, forgive my sin, because it is great.
The LORD shows His faithful followers the way they should live.

They experience His favor;
their descendants inherit the land.
The Lord's loyal followers receive His guidance, and He
reveals His covenantal demands to them.
I continually look to the Lord for help,
for He will free my feet from the enemy's net.
Turn toward me and have mercy on me, for I am alone
and oppressed!
Deliver me from my distress;
Rescue me from my suffering!
See my pain and suffering!
Forgive all my sins!
Watch my enemies,
for they outnumber me;
they hate me and
[they] want to harm me.
Protect me and deliver me!
Please do not let me be humiliated,
for I have taken shelter in You!
May integrity and godliness protect me, for I rely on You!
O God, rescue Israel from all their distress!

(NET)

These verses contain many precious truths. Thank You for Your Word that You have given to us. I bow myself to its authority today—to Your authority, my King and my God. Do as You will with me, I ask. I love You and worship You. Thank You for being my God. I am Yours.

18. A PRAYER OF PRAISE AND THANKSGIVING

Almighty Father, God of grace, let Your Name be glorified today. Your Name is superior; it is wonderful. Therefore, it is worthy to be praised and extolled. Your Name deserves honor and glory, reverence and blessing, trust and obedience. Thank You for revealing Your Name—indeed, Your Names—You have made so many of Your Names known to us to teach us various facets of Your rich, beautiful character. Truly, You are He whom my soul loves; You are the One I adore. Thank You for manifesting Yourself. You are a wise, sovereign, holy God. You are set apart in Your purity and radiance, Your goodness and love, Your truth and justice. You are so settled and steadfast in Your wisdom and strength. There is nothing that is too hard for You. Your omniscience, Your omnipotence, Your omnipresence, Your freedom, Your eternality, Your immutability: these attributes call forth the praise, wonder, and delight of Your children. We cannot understand them; they are too wonderful and too deep and too mighty for us to wrap our minds around. Thinking on You really does enlarge the soul, because Your vastness and immensity are so grand.

I love and worship You. I give myself to You and desire Your mastery and lordship over my heart, my mind, and the goings and comings of my life. How I long to honor You! I yearn to please and delight and satisfy You, yet I am so impotent. Therefore, I hope in You, in Your mercy. Continue to show Your grace and goodness to me (as You surely will!). I need You. You know this, and You will certainly undertake for me, and so I praise and thank You.

19. THE LORD JESUS CHRIST

"Jesus! The Name that charms our fears, that bids our sorrows cease; 'tis music in the sinner's ears; 'tis life and health and peace."[3]

The Lord Jesus Christ.
Our Lord Jesus Christ.
My Lord Jesus Christ.
Christ Jesus the Lord.
Christ Jesus our Lord.
Christ Jesus my Lord.
Jesus Christ the Lord.
Jesus Christ our Lord.
Jesus Christ my Lord.
Our Savior the Lord Jesus Christ.

Such power and beauty in a Name. Truly, this is *the Name* that is above every name. The Father has made it so. The Son glorified the Father perfectly on earth: He finished every task that the Father gave Him to do; He perfected obedience; He fulfilled the plan of God from before the foundation of the world; He did only the things that pleased the Father; He humbled Himself all the way to a cross-death; He was the Bringer of grace and truth; He manifested the Father exactly. He is Lord. God has highly exalted Him. God has given Him a universal throne and dominion—an everlasting kingdom. Christ Jesus our Lord will reign forever.

20. THOUGHTS FROM PSALM 40:16

May all those who seek you be happy and rejoice in you!

May those who love to experience your deliverance say continually,

"May the Lord be praised!"

Psalm 40:16 (NET)

Hallelujah! "Those who love to experience your deliverance…" Ah, this is a marvelous way to say it. Yes, we whom You have succored so often are learning to be content, and not to despair on the battlefield and in the struggles, because we have seen how the very point of difficulty, pain, and distress is the very point of rescue, salvation, deliverance. And we love to be delivered—delivered by You—delivered from internal fears, doubts, sins, and temptations, and from external dangers and snares. Delivered: not by the arm of human strength, but by Divine intervention, so that all who see can only say, "The Lord has done this. May the Lord be praised."

You can meditate on anything: a single word or phrase, a verse, a chapter, a book, a theme, a prophecy and its fulfillment, an ancient truth and its modern application, etc. You can start with something from the Word, mull over it, and bring it to bear on your life; or, you can start with something from your life—a circumstance, a question, a hurt, a joy, an interest—and bring it to the Word and seek to examine it in the light of the Word in order to see it from God's perspective. You can start with the Bible and move to the world around you, or you can start with nature and let God's creation draw your attention back to His special revelation of Himself. While this meditation obviously grew specifically out of one phrase of Scripture, every part of life provides opportunity to turn your heart and mind towards the Lord in meditation. The command to "meditate day and night" is practical, precisely because meditation can and should encompass every area of life.

Miriam K. Champlin

21. KNOWING CHRIST

O to see Him
Face to face
As men converse
Friend to Friend.
(Ex. 33)

O to know Him
Grace for grace:
Jesus, Savior,
Lamb of God.
(John 1)

O to love Him
Heart and soul,
And no other:
Only Him.
(Deut. 11)

O to please Him
Joy to joy:
Faithful service
Till life's end.
(Phil. 3)

See and know Him,
Love and please:
Life Eternal—
Knowing Christ.
(John 17)

While you may or may not appreciate poetry in general, the beauty of poetry is its conciseness. Personally, I am not a natural poet, but I do find that when I have intently meditated on a truth for weeks, or even months, I reach a point where the truth "condenses." In other words, the truth actually settles onto and into my life and, at that point, I am usually able to express it with poetic conciseness. I do not view myself as a poet, but I do think that reading and writing sacred poetry are valuable exercises/disciplines because poetry handles language and truth in a way that evokes thought and careful attention.

Miriam K. Champlin

22. A MORNING COMMUNION

As a child, I come to You. As Your child, I come to You, my Father, my own dear Father. I am Your own. You have chosen me, called me, loved me, redeemed me, and preserved me. You have given me an eternal inheritance with Christ and have sealed me with Your own Holy Spirit. Christ is my beloved and esteemed Brother, and He is my God-given Wisdom and Righteousness and Sanctification and Redemption. I will glory in this. Teach me to glory in this only. As I glory in Christ alone, let the fragrance of Christ rest upon me, and let it be dispersed abroad everywhere I go. Let Christ be seen in His beauty and worthiness. Let Him be adored. Let others see how sweet it is to trust in Jesus. I pray these things for others, but O how conscious I am that I desperately need the Spirit to cause me to believe these things and live them out. I have an implacably deceitful heart; I stand as one who needs continual grace. Thank You that You are the longsuffering Grace-Giver. I need not fear that Your capacity and willingness to give grace are less than my bountiful need for grace. Your grace will always be sufficient; yes, and in my deepest need, Your grace will super-abound. I praise this about You. I love that You are so vast and fathomless. I love that

You are so inconceivably great and so infinitely merciful. Where else could I find such steadfast love?

I throw myself at Your feet, believing that You will surely show Yourself strong on my behalf. Please give me faith and discipline to choose to believe You—not to call Your promises into question, but rather to make You famous to those around me. Please give me time with You, in the Word and in prayer. Above all things, I most fear my own distraction, my own tendency to lose sight of Your face, to tune out the Spirit's sweet, gracious voice, to bring dishonor on Your Worthy Name. I trust You, Eternal Giver of every good gift. You will never harm me. You do not deal harshly with Your children, nor will You ever begin to deal harshly with them. Thank You. Such confidence we who have fled to Jesus have! Thank You.

I kneel before You. I am Yours, today and forever. Let today be a microcosm of the eternal, sweet fellowship to which You have called me and all the others whom You have redeemed. Let me live to the praise of Your glorious grace. I love You and rejoice in You. I will obey You, by Your grace and enablement—and by Your forgiveness when I fall. Make for Yourself a great Name, because it is fitting for You to receive praise, both now and through eternal ages. Thank You for giving me armor that is perfectly suited to the battles I will fight. I put it on with wondering thanks. You are a supremely kind and wise God. I love You—very much. You love me, and when I ponder this, I find unshakeable rest and delight for my soul. Thank You.

23. IMMANUEL

Immanuel. God with us. Although He had perfect right to remain in the heavenly places with the Father, enjoying everlasting glory, displaying His perfect equality with the Father, He chose to come down to us. He did not consider His Divine prerogative a thing to be clutched but gave it up and came to earth. He humbled Himself. He, the Word, was made flesh and lived among us so that we could behold His glory—so that we could hear, see, look upon, and handle the Word. "Veiled in flesh the Godhead see; Hail th' Incarnate Deity…"[4] And so He came. God with us. God with me. My God who saves. This is like Him.

24. CHRIST: THE WORD (PART 1)

In the beginning was the Word,
And the Word was with God,
And the Word was God.
(John 1:1)

This reading and the next two work together and grow progressively. The first two are short and fairly simple, but they stair-step to the third which is fairly long and involved and will take some careful thought. Please do not read all three at once. Start with this one and just spend a day or two thinking about it. Ask questions. When is "the beginning?" Who is the Word? If "the Word was God," what are some of His attributes? Are there other Scripture passages that talk about "the Word?" Some of the questions you ask will be simple and have obvious answers. Others, you may not have an answer for at all. I find it helpful to address my questions to God and/or the Spirit—the Author(s) of the text— and view the questions and answers as a kind of dialogue between the Lord, the written Word, and myself. I try to think deeply on the immediate passage that I am considering, yet broadly, to include

Miriam K. Champlin

other passages of Scripture that will shed light on the text I am working on. Meditating on a text of Scripture must be couched in prayer. Pray over the texts that you meditate on. You are dealing with infinite truth, and unless you are divinely illumined, your finite mind and sinful heart will be unable to process it. You need the Spirit's help. So, start with this single verse, and then slowly work your way through the next two parts.

25. CHRIST: THE WORD (PART 2)

"In the beginning was the Word, and the Word
was with God, and the Word was God…And the
Word became flesh…full of grace and truth…for
the law was given through Moses, but grace and
truth came through Jesus Christ…Behold the
Lamb of God…"

(John 1:1, 14, 29).

The miraculous, unquenchable, unsearchable power
and beauty of the Incarnation. This must surely be one
of the most important truths of life: "And the Word
became flesh." What has a grander scope and bearing? How precious and transformational! "The Word
became flesh."

26. CHRIST: THE WORD (PART 3)

HIS INCARNATION

In the beginning was the Word. And the Word was with God, and the Word was God. He was in the beginning with God...(John 1:2)

...but when the fullness of time had come, God sent forth his Son, born of a woman, born under the law, to redeem those who were under the law, so that we might receive adoption as sons...(Gal. 4:4)

...for you know the grace of our Lord Jesus Christ, that though he was rich, yet for your sake he became poor, so that you by his poverty might become rich...(2 Cor. 8:9)

...Christ Jesus...though he was in the form of God, did not count equality with God a thing to be grasped, but made himself nothing, taking the form of a servant, being born in the likeness of men...(Phil. 2:6–7)

...and...became flesh and dwelt among us... (John 1:14)

...Immanuel...God with us...(Matt. 1:23)

...and we have seen his glory, glory as of the only Son from the Father, full of grace and truth... (John 1:14)

...for God so loved the world, that he gave his only Son, that whoever believes in him should not perish but have eternal life...(John 3:16)

...thanks be to God for his inexpressible gift! (2 Cor. 9:15)

(all ESV)

HIS LIFE

And Jesus increased in wisdom and in stature and in favor with God and man...(Luke 2:52)

...and Jesus went throughout all the cities and villages, teaching in their synagogues and proclaiming the gospel of the kingdom and healing every disease and every affliction...(Matt. 9:35)

...that it might be fulfilled which was spoken by Isaiah the prophet, saying, He took our illnesses and bore our diseases...(Matt. 8:17)

...for we do not have a high priest who is unable to sympathize with our weaknesses, but One who in every respect has been tempted as we are, yet without sin...(Heb. 4:15)

...He committed no sin, neither was deceit found in his mouth...(1 Pet. 2:22)

...He was teaching them as one who had authority, and not as their scribes...(Matt. 7:29)

...a Man attested...by God with mighty works and wonders and signs that God did through him...(Acts 2:22)

...in these last days, [God] has spoken to us by his Son, whom he appointed the heir of all things, through whom also he created the world. He is the radiance of the glory of God and the exact imprint of his nature ...(Heb. 1:2–3)

...no one has ever seen God; the only God, who is at the Father's side, he has made him known ... (John 1:18)

...and we have seen and testify that the Father has sent his Son to be the Savior of the world ...(1 John 4:14)

...consequently, when Christ came into the world, he said, "Sacrifices and offerings you have not desired, but a body have you prepared for me; in burnt offerings and sin offerings you have taken no pleasure. Then I said, 'Behold, I have come to do your will, O God, as it is written of me in the scroll of the book.' (Heb. 10:5–7)

(all ESV)

HIS PASSION

When the days drew near for Him to be taken up, he set his face to go to Jerusalem ...(Luke 9:51)

...And he began to teach them, that the Son of man must suffer many things and be rejected by the elders and the chief priests and the scribes and be killed, and after three days rise again ...(Mark 8:31)

...So Jesus ...said to them ...I am the good shepherd. The good shepherd lays down his life for the sheep…I am the good shepherd. I know my own and my own know me, just as the Father knows me and I know the Father; and I lay down my life for the sheep…For this reason the Father loves me, because I lay down my life that I may take it up again. No one takes it from me, but I lay it down of my own accord. I have authority to lay it down, and I have authority to take it up again…(John 10:7–18)

…the Son of Man goes as it is written of him… (Mark 14:21)

…Like a sheep he was led to the slaughter and like a lamb before its shearer is silent, so he opens not his mouth. In his humiliation justice was denied him…For his life is taken away from the earth… (Acts 8:32–33)

…So Pilate said to him, "…Do you not know that I have authority to release you and authority to crucify you?" Jesus answered him, "You would have no authority over me at all unless it had been given you from above…" (John 19:10–11)

…according to the definite plan and foreknowledge of God…(Acts 2:23)

…the chief priests and the elders persuaded the crowd to ask for Barabbas and destroy Jesus… (Matt. 27:20)

…So Pilate, wishing to satisfy the crowd, released for them Barabbas, and having scourged Jesus, he delivered him to be crucified…(Mark 15:15)

…Christ Jesus…humbled himself by becoming obedient to the point of death, even death on a cross…(Phil. 2:8)

...for...the Son of Man came not to be served but to serve, and to give his life a ransom for many... (Mark 10:45)

...For while we were still weak, at the right time Christ died for the ungodly...(Rom. 5:6)

...of first importance...that Christ died for our sins in accordance with the Scriptures, and that he was buried, and that he was raised on the third day in accordance with the Scriptures...(1 Cor. 15:3–4)

(all ESV)

And in His death, burial, and resurrection, the work of salvation was accomplished according to the eternal purpose of God!

Think of this great salvation! This is a grand redemption indeed! Worship the Word who became flesh and lived among us and died for us!

27. A PRAYER OF SURRENDER

Majesty on High, Righteous God, Holy One, Father my Father, You who are near—the One who comes to tabernacle with His people—to You I lift up my hands and my voice. "I say to [you], You are my Lord; I have no good apart from you" (Ps. 16:1–2, ESV).

I give You everything—my love, my obedience, my will, my time. I am Yours. Do what You desire with me. I lean all of me on You, because I cannot walk without You. You are life and light and hope. I adore You.

Miriam K. Champlin

28. CHRIST THE FOUNDATION

"The Church's one Foundation is Jesus Christ her Lord…"[5]

"And He is before all things…" (Col. 1:17)

The Beginning,

The First and the Last,

The Head over all things to the Church,

Christ Jesus Himself being the Cornerstone;

The Lord.

"On Christ the Solid Rock I stand: all other ground is sinking sand."[6]

When we compile lists like this, we are engaging in the 2 Corinthians 3:18 process: beholding the glory of the Lord. We are gazing on who He is, and we are trusting that, as we focus on Him, the Spirit will change us to be like Him.

29. TWO HABITATIONS

God of glory, be exalted!
Great Creator 'throned on high,
Let my praise and prayers ascending
Please Your ear inclining nigh.
Lofty is Your habitation;
Lover of the contrite soul,
Let my heart like Yours be lowly;
O descend, possess, control!

Son Anointed, I adore You,
For Your great humility—
Who, in form of God abiding,
Came in form of slave for me.
All the praise of Heav'n forsaking,
Lamb from earth's foundation slain,
Son of Man and Humble Servant,
God Incarnate lived with men.

Gracious Spirit, rich Your power
To transform the souls of men
Through the lifted veil beholding
Christ the Lord enthroned within.
As I gaze upon Christ's glory,
Mark my being—change the whole!
'Til I rise to You forever,
Helper, come, indwell my soul!

Miriam K. Champlin

Glorious Godhead, great Your goodness
In salvation's mystery—
Father, Son, and Holy Spirit
Condescend to rescue me!
Triune God, I am Your temple:
Make Your home within my soul.
Though transcendent, in Your mercy,
Come, indwell, possess, control!

The first three stanzas all correspond directly to a passage of Scripture (and the fourth is a synthesis of several). See if you can figure them out.[7] Develop the habit of taking everything back to Scripture. When you are singing in church, think of verses that go with the words you are singing. When you are reading a book, compare what you are reading with what the Bible says and pencil the phrases or references that come to mind in the margin of the book. When you are listening to someone else pray, listen for the Word in his words. You should definitely be "cross-referencing" the content of this book in your mind and stopping to look verses up. I find mental "cross-referencing" an enjoyable challenge as well as a profitable discipline.

30. PRAISE TO
THE FATHER

O God, You are my God. O Lord my God, You are very great. You are clothed with splendor and majesty. O LORD, our Lord, how excellent is Your Name in all the earth. You have set Your glory above the heavens. Lord, You have been our Dwelling Place in all generations. Before the mountains were brought forth or before You had formed the earth and the sea, even from everlasting to everlasting, You are God. So teach me to number my days and apply my heart to wisdom. I worship You, O majestic, eternal God. I worship You, Almighty Creator. I worship You, all-knowing, unchanging Father. I worship You, righteous, just, wrathful Lord. I worship You, pure, wise Ruler. I worship You, God of steadfast love. You are exalted; Your Name is great. There is no god besides You. Yours is the kingdom, the power, and the glory—forever. So teach me to hallow Your Name, to pray and live for Your kingdom, to see and know and do Your will, to depend on You and cry to You for my daily provision, for gracious forgiveness (both to and through me), and for Your protection from the evil to which I so naturally incline. Thank You. Come, worthy Lord, possess and control. You are beautiful, and I am adoring You.

31. THE SHEPHERD MEDITATIONS (PART 1)

"He will feed His flock like a shepherd; He will gather the lambs with His arm, and carry them in His bosom, and gently lead those who are with young" (Isa. 40:11). "Like a shepherd…" What analogy is God drawing? Consider shepherds in Biblical times. Who were they, and what did they do? Basically, the shepherd did everything necessary for the good of the sheep, usually at great personal cost. Figuratively and sometimes literally, the shepherd laid down his life for his sheep. What does the Shepherd want us to understand by this comparison/title? What characterized a good shepherd, and what does that teach us about the Good Shepherd?

A SHEPHERD'S FAITHFULNESS

Faithfulness. In many ways, faithfulness seems to be the core quality of a shepherd. The term "unfaithful shepherd" should sound like an oxymoron. When Eliab accused David of leaving his sheep for adventure/battle, this was a scathing, humiliating indictment (1 Sam. 17:28). "You left your sheep, and you call yourself a shepherd?" A shepherd ought to epitomize faithfulness. A true shepherd never, ever forsakes his sheep. For him, leaving the sheep to their own devices would be an atrocious, unthinkable wrong. These are his sheep, and he is their shepherd. By definition, that means that he faithfully cares for them in every regard. He knows that without him, the sheep have no hope. They depend on him for their very life, and he will not betray their trust. A shepherd is faithful.

» And is this not true of our Christ? Is He not wholly faithful? His faithfulness enables our contentment. Hebrews 13 commands us to keep our lives free from the love of money because He has said that He will never leave us. His faithful presence provides all that we need to be content and quiet. Christ is faithful. One of the four magnificent titles accorded to Him in Revelation 19 is "the Faithful and True." The Shepherd and Bishop of our souls is the Faithful Creator, and we may safely entrust the keeping of our souls to Him.

Take some time to look at the other things that the arm of the Lord is doing in Isaiah 40. This is the arm that gathers up His own and holds them close to Himself. Noticing details like this in the text will bring out the richness, the fullness, and the sweetness of what God is communicating about Himself and His relationship with us. When you are reading the Bible, always, always be on the lookout for what God says about Himself and how the truth about Him affects us.

32. THE SHEPHERD MEDITATIONS (PART 2)

A SHEPHERD'S WATCHFULNESS

Watchfulness. The keen, perpetually alert eye of the shepherd was vital to the safety and well-being of the sheep. The multiple, lurking dangers—thieves, wild animals, perilous terrain, unwholesome fodder, etc.—made watchfulness an indispensable attribute. A lax, unobservant shepherd would without doubt bring disaster upon his flock. Nor was this watchfulness simply passive awareness of the immediate environment. The watchfulness of a good shepherd entailed careful investigation and conscious thought to prepare safe and suitable routes between sheepfold and pasture. The sheep must be conducted safely in their daily journeys. The pastures must be examined for poisonous plants, thistles, and proximity to a pure, still water source. The sheep themselves must be observed for any sickness or irregularity. This occupation simply demanded an unremitting watchfulness.

» Again, this ought to remind you of what you know to be true of Christ's care of you.

Psalm 121 reminds us that the One who keeps Israel never slumbers. Hebrews calls the believer to confidence and courage based upon the Divine promise, "I will never leave you ... so we may boldly say, 'The Lord is my Helper'" (Heb. 13:5–6). The Good Shepherd never has, and never will, neglect to watch over His sheep and superintend everything that affects their lives.

33. THE SHEPHERD MEDITATIONS (PART 3)

A SHEPHERD'S PROTECTIVENESS

Fierce protection. Jesus tells us in John 10 that when danger threatens, a true shepherd stays with his sheep to face the danger. A hireling, who lacks the shepherd's love for the sheep, will choose to save his own skin, but the shepherd will be faithful to his flock. Even in times of weariness, the shepherd will be faithful in his responsibility. David, the shepherd, exemplifies such protectiveness of his sheep. At various points, he encountered both a bear and a lion. Because they attacked his flock, his wrath was aroused, and he killed them both. Nothing was going to touch his sheep without first dealing with him.

» Think, then, of Christ. Notice Acts 9:4: "Why are you persecuting Me?" Jesus was present to defend His people. Think of His ministry of intercession and how often He shields us from our own folly (usually our greatest danger). He sees all, knows all, and has all power to protect His sheep from anything that He knows to be truly harmful to them. We are the objects of His fierce, jealous protection.

34. THE SHEPHERD MEDITATIONS (PART 4)

A SHEPHERD'S LOVE

Love. A shepherd loves his sheep. He calls them all by name and leads them out. He talks with them—that is why they know his voice and follow him. He devotes himself to them. He loves them individually and collectively, and if even one of them strays, he relentlessly seeks that sheep until he finds it; he sets it on his shoulders and returns with great rejoicing to the fold. He even calls others to share in his delight: "Rejoice with me, I have found my sheep!" (Luke 15:6). He keeps count of every last one of them. Each of them is precious in his sight, and there is not a single one of them that he is willing to lose. His love is unconditional and steadfast. The sheep do not deserve his love, but they are the sure recipients of it.

» How deep the love of Jesus! There is nothing that His love has not and will not do for us. Salvation, sanctification (O consider how patient and merciful His love is with your soul!), and glorification are fully saturated with the love of Christ for His sheep. He is our very definition of love—in Him

Miriam K. Champlin

we see genuine love, pure love, holy love. His love is practically manifest throughout every day. Think of His rebukes—these stem from love. He does not want you to wander off; He would have you close by His side—He loves you. Think of His comforts: He knows your heart, and it is His delight to encourage and strengthen your inner man. Think of His gifts and His withholdings: with love, He chooses that which is best for you. O believe in Christ and His love for you! He is your Shepherd, and His every interaction with you breathes out His love for you.

35. THE SHEPHERD MEDITATIONS (PART 5)

A SHEPHERD'S LEADERSHIP

Leading. Leading is probably the primary function that comes to mind when one thinks of a shepherd: images of a shepherd with his crook going before a flock of sheep. This leading is wise and discerning. Whereas sheep choose and pursue foolish, hurtful things, the shepherd knows what is right for the sheep and leads them there. A sheep left to itself will eat harmful foliage and poison itself. An untended sheep will wander aimlessly and become entirely lost, exposing itself to the dangers of wild animals and treacherous trails, and treading the ways that lead to death. But the shepherd will lead the sheep. John 10 makes clear note of this shepherding work: "…He calls his own sheep by name and leads them out. And when he brings out his own sheep, he goes before them; and the sheep follow him, for they know his voice…" (John 10:3–4). He will lead them in paths of wholesomeness and life, keeping them from self-destructive ways, thwarting their foolish straying, taking

Miriam K. Champlin

every thought and care to safeguard and bring about the good of the sheep he loves. The shepherd leads by walking ahead, yet still very close to the sheep. He leads with the sound of his voice—remember, he loves the sheep and speaks with them, and they have grown to know and love the sound of his voice. He leads with understanding and gentleness and shows his knowledge of the sheep by considering the state of the flock. Are there sick ones, those bearing young, or young lambs? He will lead slowly so as not to hurt or lose any of them. Are certain trails unsuitable in various seasons? He will pursue alternate routes until he finds that which is best for his particular flock. He will lead with wisdom, love, and the good of his sheep at his heart.

» Turn and find that, again, no fuller, richer embodiment of this virtue has ever been seen than Christ. He is the ideal Leader, and He leads with all the gracious, compassionate, firm wisdom of a shepherd. He guides us with His Words, with the leading of His Spirit, and with His own example going before us. The prophets refer to the Lord and His people in terms of a shepherd and sheep frequently. The imagery is incredibly vivid and sweet: e.g. "They shall feed along the ways; on all bare heights shall be their pasture; they shall not hunger or thirst, neither scorching wind nor sun shall strike them, for he who has pity on them will lead them, and by springs of water will guide them" (Isa. 49:10, ESV). Divine providence ordained that many key leaders in the Scriptures had experience as shepherds, and God calls the leaders of His church shepherds as well.

There is a unique connection here that the Lord has given us for our learning, and the fullness of the shepherding imagery is never clearer than when it is seen in the life and ministry of the Lord Jesus. See how He shepherded and led the disciples, both the larger group and the twelve specifically. Observe His tender leading in His teaching; see how He never gave them more than they could bear. Despite their (and my) slowness and foolishness, He never abandoned them or allowed them to self-destruct. Peter says that with regard to the church, Christ is the Chief Shepherd—He leads His Church, His precious flock.

Miriam K. Champlin

36. THE SHEPHERD MEDITATIONS (PART 6)

A SHEPHERD'S SACRIFICE

Sacrifice. There is a high cost in shepherding. The shepherd's love and faithfulness are demonstrated in very personal, practical ways by his sacrificial lifestyle. A shepherd practices continual self-denial for the good of the sheep. It is one thing to perform a sacrificial act periodically, but living a sacrificial life is a completely different story. The shepherd uncomplainingly endures daily privation and discomfort in order to care for his sheep. The shepherd has no protection from exposure to the elements: the blazing desert sun, wind or sand storms, frigid nights, vicious predators, and treacherous terrain. The strain of constant watchfulness deeply drains the body and the mind, yet at night the shepherd does not flag in his care. After examining and counting every sheep individually and leading them into the sheepfold, the shepherd takes up his post at the entrance to the sheepfold and becomes "the door." He spends the night there: guarding and keeping the sheep, relinquishing the opportunity for deep, restful sleep by remaining with the flock, and enduring, without hesitation, the privations of broken rest, a hostile environment, and unrelenting responsibility. The personal cost is great. It is great in life, and if it led to death, the shepherd would not shrink back from dying for his sheep.

» Now you say to yourself: "They are sheep! Why, why, why would anyone do this for sheep?" No doubt, in heaven the angels are asking the same question. The most sacrificial life ever lived on behalf of the most undeserving recipients happened nearly two thousand years ago, when Christ the Good Shepherd came to earth and lived among men. He did not consider His privileges and position as something to be clung to, but gave them up to come to earth to shepherd the souls of men. He identified Himself as the Good Shepherd and both lived and died for a flock of sheep that was unthankful, unworthy, hostile, and stiff-necked. His sacrifice both in life and in death is unfathomable—it was an infinite sacrifice for infinite sin against the infinite, holy God. Christ gave His life for His sheep and now lives to lead them to everlasting glory in His Father's fold.

37. THE SHEPHERD MEDITATIONS (PART 7)

Provision. Although this is implicit in many of the other attributes of a shepherd, it is worth considering separately the provision that a shepherd makes for his sheep. The shepherd provides for the needs of his sheep. He provides thoroughly. He provides lovingly. He provides continually. He provides wisely. He provides faithfully. He provides in a timely manner. He is so well acquainted with his sheep and their ways that he can discern their needs both individually and collectively. And the shepherd is not slack or careless concerning the needs of his sheep. To him the sheep are important. Remember, he loves the sheep; he has their best interest at heart. He will do all that is necessary to provide for the needs of the sheep. He will provide food, water, pastures for rest, personal care for the sick or wounded, shelter at night or in inclement weather, protection, guidance, discipline and training, individual love and attention, yes—he himself will be their security and stay in every area of life. As long as they have the shepherd, the sheep will never need to take thought for their own lives. They must simply stay close to the shepherd, and he will provide.

» And now, O my soul, say: "The Lord is my Shepherd; I shall not want." The Lord is my Shepherd. I will never know what it is to lack what I need, for even if I am lacking something that is commonly considered a need, then at that point, my Shepherd is caring for a deeper need that requires one or more of those lesser needs to remain unfulfilled. Therefore, I will never not have what I genuinely need most. If an earthly shepherd provides for his sheep as described above, how much more shall my Lord the Shepherd provide for His own. Rest secure, O child of God; take refuge with the Shepherd and Bishop of your soul. Like a sheep, follow and adore your Shepherd, for He is your hope, your health, your Life.

38. THE SHEPHERD MEDITATIONS (PART 8)

CHILDREN OF THE HEAVENLY FATHER

Carolina S. Berg

Children of the Heav'nly Father
Safely in His bosom gather;
Nestling bird nor star in heaven
Such a refuge e'er was given.

God His own doth tend and nourish;
In His holy courts they flourish.
Like a father kind He spares them,
On His bosom warm He bears them.

Neither life nor death can ever
From the Lord His children sever;
For His love and deep compassion
Comfort them in tribulation.

Little flock, to joy then yield thee!
Jacob's God will ever shield thee;
Rest secure with this Defender,
At His will all foes surrender.

What He takes or what He gives us
Shows the Father's love so precious;
We may trust His purpose wholly—
'Tis our good for His own glory.[8]

Miriam K. Champlin

39. GLORY IN
CHRIST ALONE

But of Him you are in Christ Jesus, who became for us wisdom from God—and righteousness and sanctification and redemption—that, as it is written, "He who glories, let him glory in the LORD" (1 Cor. 1:30–31).

Some questions to ask as you meditate on this verse:

1. *What does "of Him you are in Christ Jesus" mean? What relationship is being signified?*
2. *What is God's wisdom? God's righteousness? God's sanctification? God's redemption?*
3. *How is Christ these things "for us?"*
4. *What does it mean to glory/boast in the Lord?*
5. *"As it is written"—to which Old Testament passage is this referring?*

(This is not an exhaustive list by any stretch of the imagination. They are just some starter questions to help you figure out the type of questions to ask when you are working on a passage.)

40. A MORNING PRAYER

Today, Beloved Father, may Your Name be counted holy and set apart! O that You would receive honor and worship according to what is due to Your Name. Let Your children reverence You. Please, let me reverence You. Let no action, no word, no thought of mine be dismissive of You. Let me see and seek Your eternal glory in every movement of my soul. Let no sinful arising go unrebuked and unrepented of. Please, O my God, in my life, "hallowed be Your name" (Matt. 6:9). I ask this with all the longing of my heart. I ask this knowing that by Your Holy Spirit, You can make it so. I ask this knowing that I cannot do it on my own, so I throw all of me on the mercy and merits of Christ, and I thank You that You have hidden my life in Him. He is worthy. He is the Lamb and the Lion. He is Your Son—the Son of Your good pleasure. Thank You for Jesus.

Miriam K. Champlin

41. THE LOVE OF CHRIST

"For the love of Christ controls us" (2 Cor. 5:14, ESV). This is powerful love. This is "love so amazing, so divine" that it "demands my soul, my life, my all."[9] Such is the love of Christ. Such is the love of Christ for man. Such is the love of Christ for me.

- The love of Christ drew the plan of redemption before the foundation of the world.
- The love of Christ created man in His own image for perfect delight and fellowship.
- The love of Christ mourned when man rejected His gracious dominion and fellowship.
- The love of Christ pursued a people for Himself through the cutting of covenants.
- The love of Christ held patience with a disobedient and rebellious people.
- The love of Christ sent prophets with divine messages of mercy and judgment.
- The love of Christ refused to give up on man, despite their perpetual enmity with Him.
- The love of Christ brought Him from heaven to earth.
- The love of Christ manifested itself throughout His entire life on earth:

   …As He healed the sick, comforted the distressed, and blessed the children.
   …As He ate with the publicans, wept over Jerusalem, and taught the crowds.

…As He instructed twelve unlikely disciples.

…As He endured temptation, hunger, thirst, weariness, sorrow, and loneliness.

- The love of Christ drew Him to take the form of a servant and be made like us.
- And ultimately, the love of Christ took Him to the cross.

The power and eternal purposes of the Godhead raised Christ from the dead. Now He has the power of an endless life. He lives forever to bring us near to God.

As we believe in Him, He opens our eyes and our hearts to see and know and believe the love that He has toward us. The more we see His love, the more we learn to understand the love of God that has been shed abroad in our hearts, and the more forcefully we will be controlled by it. See, the love that Christ has for us is one of the most powerful forces in the world, and yet, according to the wise paradoxes of God, small, sinful people may still fight against it and resist it. But for those who are Christ's, the love of Christ for them is the deepest and sweetest form of bondage. There is a weight of accountability and constraint that no other motivation can mimic. Guilt and fear are influential but destructive. The love of Christ is rich, full, edifying, delightful, strong, and unwavering. It will last for eternity. And for eternity, those who know Christ will be constrained by His love.

"O glorious love of Christ, my Lord Divine! That made Him stoop to save a soul like mine. Through all my days, and then in Heav'n above, my song will silence never; I'll worship Him forever, and praise Him for His glorious love!"[10]

Miriam K. Champlin

42. A PRAYER OF CONFESSION AFTER DISOBEDIENCE

Lord, did I do what You intended for me to do? I think I did not take the opportunity that You had prepared for me. I backed off. I failed to shoe my feet properly with the Gospel. Forgive me and teach me. Instruct and strengthen me and compel my wayward, selfish heart to love You and obey You: to see as You see and to act and speak as You desire. I abhor the pride and the faithlessness that I allow to steal Your glory. I mourn that I have made provision to abuse and silence the power of the Gospel. Ah, I have sinned against You. "Lord, in Your goodness build up Zion's walls; Let not my sin tear down Your glorious cause…" Yes, indeed, my Lord,

I plead for grace, O God of steadfast love;
By Your great mercy, all my sin remove.
Deeply ashamed for spurning You alone,
I stand condemned before Your holy throne.

Though You want truth and purity within,
I am unclean, conceived with inborn sin.
Purge me with blood, and wash me white as snow.
Hide my transgressions; heal my broken soul.

Create in me a spotless heart, I pray.
Take not Your Spirit! Cast me not away!
Restore to me salvation's joy anew,
Then I will teach the lost to turn to You.

Save me, O God—with blood my hands are stained!
Open my lips to praise Your righteous name.
Though You reject a thoughtless sacrifice,
My broken, contrite heart You'll not despise.

Lord, in Your goodness, build up Zion's walls.
Let not my sin tear down Your glorious cause.
May You delight in every sacrifice
Offered by sinners You have purified.

God can be just and sinners justify
For Jesus bled God's wrath to satisfy.
My sins the spikes that nailed Christ to the tree—
God's love and justice there for all to see.[11]

Thank You that there is forgiveness with You—so by Your forgiveness, unite my heart to fear You. I love You. I need You. I depend on You. I praise You.

> "Who is a God like you, pardoning iniquity and passing over transgression for the remnant of his inheritance? He does not retain his anger forever because he delights in steadfast love. He will again have compassion on us; he will tread our iniquities underfoot. You will cast all our sins into the depths of the sea" (Mic. 7:18–19, ESV).

O my God, I praise You for this truth. I praise You that in Christ I have all Your good pleasure and satisfaction. You have a wealth of patience. There is a bountifulness to all Your attributes that defies our comprehension. Shatter me with thoughts of Yourself, and then reflect Yourself in the fragments that You remold. I love You and trust You to do what You alone can do.

This beautiful Tyrpak hymn of confession based on Psalm 51 frequently rises from my heart when I have sinned and find myself needing, yet again, the gracious forgiveness of the Holy God of steadfast love. It can be sung to the tune of "Spirit of God, Descend upon my Heart."

43. THE MASTER

Was there ever such a Master? This Master and Lord washed His quarrelsome disciples' feet. This Master Himself claimed that He came not to be ministered to but to minister and to give His life a ransom for many. This Master made Himself of no reputation and took upon Himself the form of a servant. This Master is meek and lowly in heart, and when we are in His yoke, He will step into the other side of the yoke and pull with us. This Master is more faithful to the servants than the servants ever are to Him. This is the Master that, when all the other servants seem to be against us, causes us to stand. This is the wise Master who will never, ever, ever, ever not give us everything that we need to accomplish His purposes for His glory, because He will always give us Himself. This Master leads, instructs, directs, enables, helps, protects, watches, comforts, encourages, and sustains. He is not just Master: He is All. When He takes command of a life, He comes to complete and control it. Yes, Christ is everything.

Miriam K. Champlin

44. 2 CORINTHIANS 5

"The love of Christ compels us"
Laboring with eternity in view
We make it our aim to be pleasing Him
The great transaction—my sins to
Him; His righteousness to me
In this we groan—immortality—to see His Face
Sin's transfer to Christ—His payment
New creatures—in Christ
If I can live to myself, then I am not living in the reality of the love of Him who died for me and rose again.
If I am seeing Christ truly, then my life will
radically center on Him and His Person.
Longing to be with Him
Being His ambassador
Being borne along by His love
Living out my union with Him
Identifying myself as His alone.

I compiled this meditation by walking through the chapter, noting the main ideas, and loosely paraphrasing them. I read through the chapter several times, and each time through, I mined some of the thoughts that are explicit in the text. The "if" state-

ments reflect the text's implications for my life. The ideas are not in the same order as they appear in the text; they are piled one on top of each other as I added them during respective readings. Doing this kind of meditation is the idea of taking a highlighter and marking the main points of the chapter. There are several other meditations like this one throughout the book. The most extensive one is on the book of Colossians, where I went through and pulled out everything it had to say about Christ. Again, it was like taking a highlighter and marking every reference to Christ. The concept is simple, but since it is sometimes difficult to follow a train of thought well enough to highlight all of the big ideas on the first time through, this practice makes one read a text repeatedly and carefully. And that is why it is profitable.

Every time you come to one of these patterns of meditation, open your Bible and read and engage in the text of Scripture itself! You need to do this for all the meditations, but especially for the ones like this that are wedded so tightly to the very words and phraseology of a specific passage.

Miriam K. Champlin

45. ETERNALLY
WITH GOD

Lord God, thank You for bringing this universe into existence for Your glory. Thank You for creating man for fellowship with Yourself. Thank You, that when man turned his back on You, You did not leave the relationship shattered. Instead, You, having designed salvation by Your foreknowledge from before the foundation of the world, were determined to send Your own Son in the likeness of sinful flesh, and for sin. By doing so, You condemned sin—You gave it a death blow...

Christ condemned sin and fulfilled the righteousness of the law. He did that which God alone could do—He offered an acceptable, efficient, once-for-all sacrifice. He was the Lamb of God, and He took away the sins of the world. He was Christ—the Messiah—the Anointed One—the Long-awaited Savior. He came to seek and to save those who were lost. He did not count equality with God as something to be clutched, but He made Himself of no reputation and took upon Himself the form of a servant and was made in the likeness of men. In the history of man, there is nothing that compares with this Gift. Hardly anyone would die on behalf of a good man; yet even if that were to happen, no one would naturally die on behalf of an evil person—no one except the God-Man Jesus.

And that is what happened: God demonstrated His love toward us by sending Christ to die for us when we were still sinners.

Christ's death for us when we were still in our sin is also how we know that God will surely complete the work that He has begun in us. After all, He is the One who did not spare His own Son, but gave Him up for us all. How would God not, with Christ also, freely give us all things—fully accomplish the great salvation that He started? God will not be slack. He will not tire. He will not suffer His faithfulness to fail. He will not forsake His own. He will bring many sons to glory—just as He has perfected their Captain. They will all stand spotless and blameless, holy and loving in His sight one day. They will all look like Christ. Even those who reject Christ will ultimately bow to Him as God's fulfills His promise to the Son: I will make Your enemies Your footstool. When God at last, in ultimate triumph, pronounces that Jesus Christ is Lord, every knee will bow, every mouth will agree with God, sin will be banished, and righteousness will reign. Final justice will be accomplished: Jesus will be enthroned, and He will reign forever and ever as King of kings and Lord of lords. As for the people He died to redeem, the many sons that He brought to glory, they will serve Him; they will see His face; His Name will be written on their foreheads; and they will sing the new song of the redeemed: "You are worthy..." God will keep His own with Him for all eternity, and His own will spend eternity praising and adoring Him, because He is worthy.

47. LONGING FOR
HIS RETURN

My Jesus, I long for the day when the new song will begin eternally: "You are worthy..." (Rev. 4:11). There will be no end to the homage that is paid to You. Your dominion will at last extend universally again, all will bow, and Your own will glorify You forever. Haste that day! And in the meantime, receive this offering of praise from my mouth. I love You very much.

The thought of the return of Christ and being in His presence eternally ought to thrill your heart. If it does not, you need to ask God to grow a longing for and an anticipation of Christ's return in your heart. 2 Corinthians 5 says that the Spirit is the One who teaches us to yearn for our eternal home. You might find it helpful to spend some time in passages like Titus 2:11–15; Matthew 24:40–46; 1 Thessalonians 4:16–18; Revelation 22:4–5, and others that speak jubilantly of being with the Lord.

47. A POEM OF GRATEFUL ADORATION

Jesus, Prize our hearts adoring,
Jesus, joy and peace restoring,
Jesus Christ, our souls outpouring,
We will worship You.

Hear Your children's earnest pleading:
"Come, O Lord, Your kingdom bringing."
Come, Your people's hearts are seeking;
Long we've looked for You.

Christ, on You our hearts' relying
For our every need's supplying;
You alone are satisfying;
We will boast in You.

Miriam K. Champlin

48. A PRAYER OF WORSHIP AND COMMITMENT

Dear Lord Jesus, Risen, Triumphant Savior, Kings of kings and Lord of lords, Ruler of the kings of the earth, all praise to You! You are the Christ—the long-awaited Messiah, the Conqueror, the Vanquisher of the power of sin, death, and Satan. Exalt Your Name, for You rightly have the Name that is above every name. This highest of names was given to You by the Father because of Your obedience and cross work. Thank You for dying for me. Thank You for the far-reaching, indeed, universally powerful and glorious implications of Your death, burial, and resurrection. Thank You for prophecy fulfilled, atonement accomplished, peace between Jew and Gentile, access into the Holiest, prayer to the Father in Your Name, the Spirit poured out on believers, and the quickening of souls dead in trespasses and sins. Thank You for choosing to use this means—the plan of salvation crafted before the foundation of the world, fulfilled in absolute perfection by the Lamb slain from the foundation of the world—to display for all eternity how rich the Father is in grace, how kind His mercy is, and how even eternity will be too short to adequately adore Him. Thank You for the Father's revealing of Himself through You. Thank You that we may genuinely, legitimately, and eternally be children of God, and know You, serve You, and worship You. Hallelujah!

Reign in splendor over my life, O Master and King. Have all of me and do as You will with me. Please fill my mind to think Your thoughts after You. Direct my heart to love what You love, hate what You hate, and feel as You feel toward others. Tune my ears to understanding of truth, to discernment in conversation, and most of all, to obedience to the Spirit. Open my eyes to righteousness and close them to that which, if it entered, would defile. Take my mouth and set a watch over my words; seal my lips to that which is not fitting. Possess the doings of my hands and feet, the reflection of my countenance, the inflow and outflow of all of my life today. Do this, I pray, for Your Name and glory's sake. I love You and gladly yield myself to You. Be exalted forever and ever. I need You and trust You. Thank You for being mine, and I Yours.

The importance of praise. When you pray, it is of utmost importance that you discipline your mind and heart to praise and thank God. Often you will not "feel" like praising Him. We are naturally ungrateful people, so praise is not always spontaneous, even to the redeemed. Make this a priority! Few things dry up one's walk with God more quickly than lack of praise.

Let your requests flow out of your praise. As you acknowledge the greatness and glory of God, the Spirit will be calibrating your heart to pray in accordance with the character and ways of God. It is only when you see God in the proper perspective that you are able to approach Him with the proper reverence, confidence, and intimacy. So be diligent in praise and adoration, and make your requests with thanksgiving to God.

Miriam K. Champlin

49. A MEDITATION FOR RENEWING THE MIND

My mind needs cleansing, so I come, dear Master, to gaze on Your face and admire Your beauty and purity:

> I am the true vine, and My Father is the vine-dresser. Every branch in Me that does not bear fruit, He takes away; and every branch that bears fruit, He prunes, that it may bear more fruit. You are already clean because of the word which I have spoken to you. (John 15:1–3)

> I am the resurrection and the life. He who believes in Me, though he may die, he shall live and whoever lives and believes in Me shall never die. Do you believe this? (John 11:25–26)

> I am the light of the world. He who follows Me shall not walk in darkness, but have the light of life. (John 8:12)

> I am the living bread which came down from heaven. If anyone eats of this bread, he will live forever. (John 6:51)

> I am the door. If anyone enters by Me, he will be saved, and will go in and out and find pasture. (John 10:9)

> I am the way, the truth, and the life. No man comes to the Father except through Me. (John 14:6)

I am the good shepherd. The good shepherd gives His life for the sheep. (John 10:11)

I am He who lives and was dead, and behold, I am alive forevermore. Amen. And I have the keys of Hades and of Death. (Rev. 1:18)

I am the Alpha and the Omega, the Beginning and the End, the First and the Last." (Rev. 22:13)

We all know what it is like to try to pray, but find that our minds are totally distracted and our thinking clogged with "stuff." The best way to cleanse and renew the mind is through "the washing of water by the word" (Eph. 5:26). When my mind is clouded and dusty, I find that the most effective way to receive cleansing and refreshment is to go to what the Word says about Christ, and simply let the truth about Jesus wash over my heart and mind and clear out the debris. When I am in a place of mental fuzziness and distraction, this kind of meditation is not something that I "feel" like doing, but it is what my spirit and mind need. It sets my heart and my thinking right and restores a spirit of praise to God.

Miriam K. Champlin

50. "NO MAN EVER SPOKE LIKE THIS MAN"

I am considering, dear Savior and Lord, the beauty and integrity of the words of Your mouth. Well did the people in the synagogue in Nazareth wonder at the words that You spoke. Well did the multitudes marvel at the authority with which You taught. It is true, as the officers of the chief priests observed, "No man ever spoke like this Man!" (John 7:46). Because You are the Word of God and the Grace of God and the Wisdom of God, Your speech was always with grace, seasoned with salt. Your answer to every man who spoke with You was full of truth and understanding. Your words were purposeful and effective. They were pleasing to the Father. Often, Your words were few. At other times, they were many. They were gauged and meted out in accordance with Your purposes, Your glory, and Your righteousness.

Your speech was like this. O that mine may be made like Yours.

51. THE COLOSSIANS PORTRAIT OF CHRIST

How does Colossians portray Christ? Who
is Christ as revealed in this book?

The Son of His love—the Ruler of a kingdom
of light, filled with people redeemed out of the
power of darkness and transferred out of its kingdom and power by the power of His blood.

The Image of the invisible God, the Firstborn—
the Foremost in rank, power, and authority.

The Creator (and, just so we do not miss the grand-
ness of this, it is listed for us: things in heaven and in
earth; things seen and unseen; and the whole scope
of human authority and government)—Creator of all
and Recipient of all the praise and acclaimed beauty.

Christ—before all and causing all to hold together.

He is the Head; He is the Beginning;
He is the Preeminent One.

It was pleasing for all the fullness to dwell in Him;
God the Father placed all His rich fullness in Christ.

The One who made peace with His blood
on the cross; He reconciled all things to
Himself—yes, He reconciled even me.

Wonderful Savior!

Miriam K. Champlin

By taking the eternal punishment, by tasting death for every man, He reconciled us. He intends to present us holy, blameless, and irreproachable to the Father.

Christ brought the Gospel.

And He is the Hope that the Gospel brings—He Himself is the Hope of glory, and He is the One that we proclaim with teaching and admonition, as we labor to be like Him, working to present men mature in the presence of God. Christ is also the One who provides the energizing for this task.

Christ: all the treasures of wisdom and knowledge are hidden in Him ... therefore we are to be captivated by Him.

Walk—in Christ. Be rooted—in Christ. Be grounded—in Christ. Be built up—in Christ. Grow in thankfulness—in Christ. Because all the fullness of Deity is in Christ, and we also are in Christ. Yes, we are in Christ the Head, the Chief, the Foremost of all principality and power.

In Christ, we have put off the body of the sins of the flesh; we are set apart by the circumcision of Christ.

We have been identified with Christ by His baptism; in Christ we have died and risen again to walk in newness of life. God has seen fit to set His mighty power to work in us to raise us from the dead together with Christ.

Through the cross-death of Christ, God blotted out the decrees against us and nailed the document of accusations against us to the cross of Christ.

Christ is the Triumphant One who leads captive the principalities and powers—those who so glibly thought that they had triumphed over Him in His death.

This is so, so incredibly beautiful! See the power and majesty of the Triumphant, Conquering Christ! Only a Name like His could accomplish this!

The whole body is Christ's. He is the Head. From Him we are all knit together, and as we live in Him, we grow.

We are dead with Christ—100 percent dead to the world, no longer subject to it in any way, shape, or form.

Those of us who are risen with Christ must pursue the things that pertain to heaven where He is, because our death necessitates our identification with Him. He has hidden our lives in His own.

Christ is our Life.

Christ will return and manifest Himself to us again.

When Christ returns, we will be with Him.

Christ, and being with Christ, is our motive for sanctifying our lives here— for rooting out the sin in our lives.

Christ is All and in all.

Christ's forgiveness of us is the ground of our forgiving those around us.

It is Christ's Word that is to live in us
richly, and in His Name we are to carry
out our actions with full thanksgiving.

It is Christ that we serve; He is the Ultimate Master.

To be imprisoned for speaking of Christ is worth it.

Christ—exalted, preeminent.

Christ—glorious, full.

Christ—worthy, triumphant.

Christ only. Christ supreme.

This is the Colossians portrait of
Christ. Truly, He is Lord.

*For this meditation, I simply went through the
book of Colossians and looked for everything it
said explicitly about Christ and some of the explicit
implications and recorded them briefly yet thoughtfully and worshipfully. And it was very sweet.*

*You will notice a couple of places in the meditation
where I inserted a comment in italics. That was the
spontaneous outflow of praise from my heart as I
walked through the text and the truth about Christ
made my heart rejoice. Let your soul exult as the
Spirit opens your soul to know God better. As the
Truth Teacher illuminates your mind and warms
your affections, respond in worship.*

52. A PRAISE TO THE CREATOR

Creator God, You make such beautiful things, and I am grateful. Grateful for the senses to take in Your revelation and grateful for a relationship with You that enables me to appreciate Your revelation. Thank You. Thank You for revealing Yourself. Thank You for showing the edges of Your nature and ways in the created order. You show Your abundant diversity by the sweeping scope of the things You made. Animals: the sponge on the ocean floor, the giraffe, the dragonfly, the turtle, the oyster, the shark, the chipmunk, and so on. Plants: mosses, lichens, cypress trees, tomato plants, Venus fly-traps, pines, deciduous trees, annuals, biennials, perennials, algae, vines, shrubs, sequoias, coconut trees, oak trees, pumpkin vines, cornstalks, the grains, and on and on. Just in the bird kind: owls, sparrows, woodpeckers, ostriches, hummingbirds, eagles, vultures, blue jays, parrots, penguins, wrens, chickadees, doves, chickens, emus, nuthatches, ducks, kingfishers, weaver birds, pelicans, birds of paradise, mockingbirds, swallows, crows, quail, peacocks, cuckoos, puffins, scissor-tailed flycatchers, loons, catbirds, hawks, nightingales, parakeets, partridges, swans, condors, pigeons, robins, sandpipers, seagulls, crossbills, finches, geese, kookaburras, nighthawks, cockatoos, starlings, larks,

Miriam K. Champlin

roadrunners, albatrosses—and all those are just a few. Who but You? No one except You has that creativity and power. No one except You has such diverse ways of displaying beauty within a single life form. You did not content Yourself by creating myriads of kinds only; You put stunning variety into each kind. I marvel at that and thank You for the privilege of enjoying it.

We could discuss food. We could describe colors. We look around at the people You have created and are astonished at the remarkable range of gifts and abilities that You have dispensed. Even a marred image of You in humanity is still breath-taking. No one like You! O God, there is no one like You! Look at the disciplines: music, mathematics, language, art, science, athletics, architecture/design. In each, You have left Your fingerprints, and Your fingerprints are astounding. They point us to eternal truths about You, Your greatness, Your unchangeableness, Your beauty, Your orderliness. Your works declare Your glory; they shout Your praises. And all this is but general revelation—that which You have displayed to every person. Just when we would think the chorus of praise could not grow any louder or more joyous, we turn to consider special revelation: the Holy Scriptures and the Son of Man—both opened to us through the Spirit. What more can we say? Our words are insufficient and our tongues are stammering. I lift my eyes, my hands, my heart to You. I worship You, Great Creator, Transcendent God, Immanent Father. Thank You for making Yourself known. Of all that You have given to me, You Yourself are Your own best gift. Thank You for letting me know You.

53. JESUS THE LORD

"He is Lord;
He is Lord.
He is risen from the dead,
And He is Lord.
Every knee shall bow,
Every tongue confess,
That Jesus Christ is Lord."[12]
God has given Him the Name above every name: He
    is Lord.
His throne is eternal.
His scepter is a scepter of righteousness.
There is no end of His kingdom and glory.
Yes. He is Lord.

Miriam K. Champlin

54. TO GLORY IN KNOWING GOD

You say, "Glory in Me."
But here I stand:
Glorying in folly that I call "wisdom,"
      poverty that I claim as "wealth,"
      and impotence that I have termed "strength."
I foolishly deem my position to be secure.

But You will not leave me to my own devices.
You strip and crush my life until I am
      undone,
        broken,
          desolate,
            laid in the dust,
              wounded,
                disconsolate,
                  shattered,
                    poor and needy.
              Hopeless, apart from You.

I begin to know seeking with the whole heart,
      hungering and thirsting after righteousness.
Your Spirit teaches me.
You allow me to know Your love
shed abroad in my now-open heart.

You have taken away everything—
Everything that I had clutched and boasted in—
And You have jealously claimed me to be Yours alone.

And now You say, "Glory in Me."
But still I recoil.
I am too shallow to take You at Your Word.
I think that I must manufacture righteousness on my
own ...somehow ...
I still fail to recognize that
You are who You say You are.
You are the God who exercises
  loving-kindness,
   forgiveness,
    mercy.
The God who delights in steadfast love.
The God who takes pleasure in manifesting Himself.

And so You take me still lower:
  revealing pride,
   touching fears,
    uprooting self,
     illuminating sin,
      warring against everything that
      keeps me in bondage to myself,
You take my life to the cross.
You cause its shadow to fall across my entire being,
and I am left
  silent,
   humbled to the dust,
    yielded,
     resting in You alone,

Miriam K. Champlin

> slowly lifting my eyes to gaze at You,
>> weeping with a joy that crushes,
>>> mourning under a burden
>>> that restores.

Then You say, "Glory in Me."

And now I understand.

I allow You to take my hand and draw me to my feet.

I stand before You whole—though I have never been so weak and empty.

I cannot take my eyes off Your face.

I throw back my shoulders,
> and begin to sing of You with a confidence that comes from knowing You.

But then, in the midst of my song, I realize what You have actually done for me:

You have let me know You.

And I do know You now.

My song of You is flowing from a heart that is weeping uncontrollably at the sight of

Your Person and Your ways—who You are and what You have done.

I am just starting to see Your perspective on all of this:

I am who I am. I am a finite, sinful, created being. I am nothing apart from You.

And that is okay. In fact, it is irrelevant.

Because You are who You are. And You have determined to make me know You, and You are determined to bring Yourself glory.

You have spared nothing to accomplish Your purpose.

What You have done to me and for me has brought You glory and pleasure,

and as I accept the riches and the righteousness
that You lavish on me,
I can live to the praise of the glory of Your grace.

This is what it means to glory in You:
It is to not insult Your fullness by living in my own
resources.
It is to experience continually my life being brought to
the foot of the cross,
        being marked by its shadow.
It is to be confident in that position,
        knowing that You are Everything—literally
        Everything—to me.

So when You say, "Glory in Me,"
I can rightfully boast in the one thing that I have the
least right to boast in: Knowing God.
I can lift up my head and sing…about my Savior.
Yes, I can glory…in knowing You,
And You alone.

55. WORSHIP-PROMPTED OBEDIENCE

Glorious Heavenly Father, God sitting upon the throne, receive the jubilantly solemn worship of our souls—the earnest exuberance of our beings in response to the sight of You enthroned in all Your worthiness and might. God of grace, Eternal One, thank You for Your Word—Your Truth. Thank You for the teaching of Your Holy Spirit and for giving me understanding. I praise You! I join my voice with the millions of those whose faith is sight, for though I do not see Him, I too love the Lamb. Yet if I love the Lamb, it is solely because He first loved me, and so again I must adore and return thanks, for from Him and through Him and to Him are all things. So "let my life show forth Your praise,"[13] dear Lord. Blessed, Holy Master,

Lord, to Your servant now impart
The grace to serve with humble heart
And single eye concerned alone
To please the One upon the throne.
Let neither idle thoughts attract,
Nor sinful fear of man distract
And shift my gaze e'en subtly.
Dear Lord, from me deliver me.

I love You, my God. Rule my life. Do as You will, only be pleased and glorified in my life.

56. ROMANS 6

No obligation to sin
The reality of union with Christ
Walking in newness of life
Slave to righteousness
Sin has no more dominion
If I sin, it is a voluntary "tax" given to an ille-
gitimate lord, an utter imposter.
If I live to myself, I am ignoring my union
with Christ and worshipping myself.
Bearing fruit to righteousness
Fleshing out holiness
Obeying the Word
Identifying with Christ

Miriam K. Champlin

57. THE COMING ONE

One of the main functions of the Old Testament is to display the sufficiency of Christ. In the Old Testament, there was always something lacking, always the need for something more, always forward momentum to a time when there would be someone who would _____

_____.

Even though there was a people with a special relationship to God, and though it was enough for them to walk by faith, there was always a waiting for something more, always a looking to the future for One who would come. The old covenant is a covenant of expectation. There must be more.

Think of some of the grand pictures of Christ in the Old Testament:

The One who would crush the serpent's head,

The Door,

The Lamb that God would provide for Himself—the Final Sacrifice for sin.

The Perfect Priest,

The Perfect King/Leader, and

The Perfect Prophet.

Christ is all of these.

He was the Answer

to the all the questions,

all the hopes,

all the desires of His people.

Christ was and is the Answer.

Christ. He fulfilled it all.

Christ. He was the Sufficient One.

Christ. He was Enough.

Christ. He was the Completion of all expectation.

Christ alone.

The New Testament is so rich, because it is the revelation of Jesus Christ: the One who would come and fill all in all.

58. CHRIST'S FULFILLMENT OF THE OLD TESTAMENT

Christ…Think on Him as the Grand Theme of the Old Testament—the One who brought into perfect unity the whole scope of its prophecy and revelation.

Christ…The Master and Servant and Fulfiller of the law—the law whose very function was to be a schoolmaster to bring us to Christ.

Christ…Sent by God the Father, in the fullness of time, to earth.

He came to earth and was obedient in all things.

He loved righteousness and hated iniquity.

He did not do His own will, but the Father's.

He offered Himself upon the cross, to bear the sins of many.

He died at the hands of cruel and unrighteous men.

And yet, He was already the Lamb, slain from the foundation of the world.

And now He lives!

59. CHRIST IN ISAIAH

Isaiah has so many beautiful, precious portraits of Christ. The names of Christ and prophecies concerning the Offspring to come are manifold and fascinating.

> There shall come forth a Rod from the stem of Jesse, and a Branch shall grow out of his roots. The Spirit of the Lord shall rest upon Him, the Spirit of wisdom and understanding, the Spirit of counsel and might, the Spirit of knowledge and of the fear of the Lord. His delight is in the fear of the Lord, and He shall not judge by the sight of His eyes, nor decide by the hearing of His ears; but with righteousness He shall judge the poor, and decide with equity for the meek of the earth; He shall strike the earth with the rod of His mouth, and with the breath of His lips He shall slay the wicked. Righteousness shall be the belt of His loins, and faithfulness the belt of His waist.
>
> Isaiah 11:1–5

Is any but Christ like this?

It challenged me that Christ was distinguished by the fear of the Lord. He is the *Lord*. He always did that which pleased the Father. Yet He was marked by the fear of the *Lord*. He lived in the continual awareness of the presence and power of God. O that I might be like my Lord in this!

Beautiful Savior, Lord of my heart, I am loving You and looking to You. You alone are worthy of worship.

Miriam K. Champlin

60. NEW LIFE IN CHRIST

Lord Jesus, Risen, Conquering Son, Your endless victory is excellent! It is a superlative victory—decisive, final, glorious. I praise You for so triumphing over every foe, for thus establishing Your preeminence, for thus putting to open shame all the powers that fought to keep us in bondage. Truly, in Christ is new life indeed. In Christ, the dead are made to live; the weak are made strong; the unrighteous are clothed with righteousness; the hopeless are given eternal, unfading hope; the perishing are rescued; the fallen are lifted up; the depraved are redeemed; the bound are set at liberty; the corrupt are made holy; the joyless made to sing a new song of praise; the disobedient and unbelieving become dear, obedient children: this is eternal salvation—eternal life—knowing the Father and the Son through the Spirit who has made us one with the Father, with Christ, and with our fellow-believers.

61. CONFESSING DISTRACTION

My own Lord, it is over halfway through our hour together, and I have been rather idly distracted in my prayers and have not given my whole mind and soul over to this great task that You have put before me. Forgive me for showing irreverence by my casualness and my willingness to give You a half-hearted offering. Ah, I am ashamed...please, my Lord, pardon my sin, remember it no more, and quicken me to approach You rightly in the Name of my Lord Jesus. I love You. I extol Your gracious quickness to forgive. Thank You for dealing mercifully and so firmly and righteously with my soul. I make much of Your goodness to the children of men. There is none like You!

Amy Carmichael offers some helpful advice on the subject of distraction in prayer: "Don't give up in despair if no thoughts and no words come, but only distractions and inward confusions. Often it helps to use the words of others, making them one's own. Psalm, hymn, song—use what helps most" (Edges of His Ways, pg. 196). This bit of encouragement and counsel has strengthened me countless times. You will notice that I have often used lines from

Miriam K. Champlin

Scripture, lines from hymns or poems, quotations, and ideas from others. Allow the contributions of other saints to strengthen and focus your walk with the Lord.

62. A MEDIATOR

Jesus Christ: a Faithful Intercessor and Mediator to stand in the gap.

Now, "let us draw near" (Heb. 10:22), because Christ has made it possible for us to enter the presence of God Himself.

This meditation is basically a concise synthesis of Hebrews 8–10. Hebrews 10:22 would be a "capstone verse" (see the note on 7b) of those three chapters. Basically, instead of walking you through Hebrews 8–10 to stir up your thoughts, I am giving you the finished product. I highly recommend that you read these chapters thoughtfully with this end focus in mind. "Let us draw near" is the application that the author of Hebrews is going to draw after he finishes outlining the majesty, sufficiency, and eternality of Christ's High Priesthood.

Miriam K. Champlin

63. HE IS

Christ is beautiful.
He is grand.
He is majestic.
He is glorious.
He is rich.
He is strong.
He is infinite.
He is faithful.
He is gracious.
He is righteous.
He is lovely.
He is Lord.
Christ.
Christ is my Lord.
He is my Keeper.
He is my Beloved.
He is my Life.
He is my Shield.
He is my Righteousness.
He is my Wisdom.
He is my Redemption.
He is my Rock.
He is my Teacher.
He is my Friend.
He is my God.
Christ. Emmanuel. Savior. Sustainer. Master.
Supplier. Enabler. Jesus. Light of the world.

64. A PRAYER OF PRAISE AND THANKSGIVING

O my Lord, You are so rich. Your resources are incomparable in every regard. When I consider You and Your great wealth, I am humbled and encouraged. You are rich in mercy. You are rich in grace. Rich in love. Rich in long-suffering. You are rich in physical resources: money, food, clothing, and shelter. You give strength to labor. You provide the conveniences of life—a computer, vehicle, refrigerator, stove, laundry machines, vacuum cleaners, etc. You are rich in Your knowledge of exactly what we need and when we need it. You are rich in wisdom in giving and taking away. You are rich in intangible resources such as comfort, understanding, chastening, counsel, love, rebuke, and teaching. You are rich in faithful servants whom You use to do Your work. Thank You for all these things. I love You very much and praise Your fullness.

65. GOD WITH US

Glorious Jesus, Anointed One, Ultimate Prophet, Priest, and King: be glorified. Worthy, righteous, Holy One, Son of God, You are like the Father in His very essence. You are God the Son: God very God and Son of Man. You became like us for the suffering of death. You were tempted as we are and subjected to infirmity—weariness, thirst, hunger, pain. As Deity, You partook of humanity, for humanity's good. You are Emmanuel: God with us. O let Your Name linger on our tongues and burn in our minds.

Reader, meditate on this: God—with—us. God with us. God with us: full of grace and truth, doing among us the works that no other had ever done. God with us: speaking with authority, going about doing good, commanding winds, waves, and unclean spirits, and receiving perfect obedience from them. God with us: having compassion on the sick, the weak, and the hopeless. God with us: making the Father known. God with us. Jesus.

Yet, it was necessary that He go away, so that we could receive Another…Another One like Him. One who would dwell with us and be in us. The very Holy Spirit of God. Him, too, we have received. All praise to the Giver of good gifts!

66. THE KING

The Ideal King.
The Ultimate King.
The Righteous King.
The Eternal King.
The King of Israel.
The King from the line of David.
The King to whom the nations come.
The King of the everlasting kingdom.
The King of kings and Lord of lords.

Eternal Sonship and dominion. A throne forever. The scepter of righteousness. The earth for a footstool. Habitation in the high places. Divine anointing. The Name above every name. All the prerogatives of Deity. The final Fulfillment of the Old Testament hopes and promises. As Nathanael said, "Rabbi, You are the Son of God! You are the King of Israel!" (John 1:49).

The history of Israel bears testimony to the need for a perfect king. The pages of the Kings and Chronicles tell the dismal tale of sinful, incompetent, short-lived earthly dynasties. The Davidic covenant bears a continual message of hope, but the reality of life and kings in the Old Testament remained bleak, well nigh hopeless. "O Come, O Come, Emmanuel" is a song that captures well the mournful longing, to which one is brought at the end of the Old Testament. Every human ruler has

Miriam K. Champlin

failed, and hope has been dashed. The hope of Israel seems futile. God has sent His last prophet, and His last prophet's last words involved cursing, and now God is silent.

But God is faithful, and His covenant with David is everlasting. Where is the son who is to reign?

So in the fullness of time, God sent His Son. He was a King, but His own rejected Him. They would have none of His kingdom and righteousness. They crucified Him.

The pagan governor is the one who put the inscription "King of the Jews" above His head as the record of His crime, but the people clamored against this accusation and claimed Caesar as their king.

But around the time of His death, the King had said that His kingdom was not of this world, and the nation of Israel had not faith to see the unseen.

And they killed their King—the ideal King—the One that their Scriptures would have taught them to hang all of their hopes on, if they had read the Scriptures with eyes to see, ears to hear, and a heart to believe.

Yet nothing can or will hinder the rise to power that this God-appointed King has begun. He conquered death and rent the grave. He wrested the sting away from death and the victory away from the grave, for He has the power of an endless life.

Regardless of the reception He received on His first advent on earth, He will come again. And this time, every eye will see His kingliness. Every knee will bow to Him. Every tongue will acknowledge His Lordship. He will destroy in an instant the kingdoms and dominions of this present evil world and the principalities and powers that dictate them. He will establish His throne throughout the universe and of His kingdom there will be no end. He will make all the former things to pass away. He will make all things new. He will complete the renewing work that He began in His own citizens when they first entered His kingdom, having repented of the enmity they once bore to Him and His Father. (For, by the blood of His cross, a number of the children of men were given power to become the sons of God, and if sons, then heirs: heirs of God together with the King.)

The King has chosen to exalt His worthiness and magnify His greatness eternally by raising up an entire people of kings and priests, who are to be like small prisms to show forth what He is like. This called-out body of His worshippers will image Him to the world throughout time and eternity.

He is the only One worth imaging. He is the King. He has the right to be adored and imitated and worshipped and loved. We owe Him everything, because He is the Creator, the Redeemer, the Sustainer, the Intercessor, the Lover, the Resurrection, the Head, the Consummator. He is the King. He is the Absolute Despot and He will be so forever and ever.

Of His kingdom there will be no end. He will reign eternally: the King of kings.

67. JESUS IS WORTHY

Jesus Christ.

The Lamb of God slain from the foundation of the world.

The Infinite Sacrifice for infinite sin against the Infinite God.

The One who is living and was dead and is now alive forevermore, having the keys of death and hell. And He is the King of those who are kinging and the Lord of the ones lording.

Jesus Christ the Lord.

68. A MORNING PRAYER

To You I lift up my eyes, O You who dwell in the heavens. I am gratefully conscious of my need for You, for Your fear-invoking forgiveness, for Your strength, for the streams of grace and steadfast love that will sustain me today in all that You choose for me. I am grateful for Your wisdom and Your mind, for the armor that You supply, for Your enablement to be a minister of the new covenant—whether a minister of death to death or of life to life. O please publish the Gospel through my life today! O that I may love to tell the Story like You love to tell the Story.

I praise You for Your nearness—that You are transcendent yet immanent. I praise You for making Yourself known; You are the God who is manifest, even to the point of becoming flesh and living with us. I praise You for Your faithfulness—You are the True One; Your faithfulness is not conditioned or reactive. Rather, it *is*: You *are* faithful.

Lord God my Father, Lord Jesus my Brother, Holy Spirit my Teacher of Truth, I kneel in worship and devotion, in praise and surrender. Please come and take control. Do as only You can do. By Your grace, I will obey You, and I put on the armor that You have supplied. Thank You for being with me to cause me to stand. I need You so, so much, and I find that You are a very present Help. I love You because You love me. Thank You for being my God. My soul takes rest in You. Be glorified today.

Miriam K. Champlin

69. PSALM 84

"No good thing will He withhold"
Nothing
Nothing good that He has not given to me
Everything in my life works for my good.
If I can imagine anything good outside of
Christ, then I am only imagining it.
If I am not satisfied with what He has given into
my life, then I am not seeing Him clearly.
Trusting in His "muchness"
Living out of His goodness
Loving His fellowship
Worshipping Him
Finding Him to be my Sun and Shield
If I do not believe that even one day with Him is
better than a thousand days anywhere else, then
I have not truly tasted of His grace and glory.
If I am not happy, then I am not truly trusting Him.

70. SALVATION

All praise to You, O Son of God, when
guilty sinners, ransomed, come
And, now—illumined, pardoned, freed—
stand righteous, justified, redeemed;
For 'tis Your blood so freely shed, that
tore the barrier veil in two,
And 'tis Your death that conquered Death
and snatched the vict'ry from the grave.

All hail to You, Atoning One, God's
wrath on You fully outpoured
Is left no more for us to drink, but
rather life and peace with God.
Propitiation bought with blood, in sub-
stitution reckoned mine;
Elected, yes, and made a son, for men
through Gospel drink of Grace.

Eternal praise, Eternal Lamb—
through endless ages we'll adore
In holiness imputed ours when we
received the Gift of gifts.
Sin's full remission purifies Your
new creation now made one
With You, O God, through Christ the
Son whom we confess as Lord alone.

Miriam K. Champlin

Before the world's foundations were,
God planned His mercy to display.
And God took thought, took flesh, took
wrath; He suffered, died, and rose again.
He reconciled wayward men in mighty
wisdom through a cross,
And Christ, once made a curse for us, now
brings His blood-bought brothers home.

71. THE LAMB OF GOD

Even the earliest chapters of Scripture begin to reveal truth that "without shedding of blood, there is no remission" (Heb. 9:22). When Adam and Eve sinned, God killed a lamb and made a covering for them, and from that point on—Cain and Abel, Noah, Abraham, Isaac, Jacob—we see sacrifices offered, blood shed, and a covering made for sin. And yet there was no finality. The question remained: What can take away my sin?

The Old Testament records the covenant of the law that God gave to His people on Mount Sinai by the hand of Moses. This covenant contained a system of feasts, ceremonies, and sacrifices to be performed in specific ways, at specific times during the worship of Yahweh, the true and living God. The LORD required His people to approach Him through sacrifices, so that they might come with clean hands and a pure heart. Both a proper sacrifice and a reverent heart toward Yahweh were necessary in order to please Him. But still this system—intricate, God-designed, and significant though it was—could not effect the cleansing of sin. The question remained: What can take away my sin?

The question hung in the air and in the hearts of true worshippers for hundreds of years. Millions of gallons of blood were shed. Rivers upon rivers of blood flowed from the Tabernacle and then the Temple.

Millions of spotless lambs, bulls, and goats were sacrificed for sin, but there was no finality, no permanent sacrifice, no cleansing of sin. And the people yearned, they groaned, cried out, and mourned for a final sacrifice—a sacrifice that would effectively crush sin and its dominion. Those who loved God increasingly ached for His redemption, and they questioned in agony of soul: What can take away my sin?

Throughout this entire time, however, as the centuries dragged on, God was sending His people messages of hope—a Savior would come. God, in various times and in various ways, spoke to His worshippers and promised them salvation. Sin would not always have, as it were, the upper hand. One day there would be a sacrifice to take away sin.

Then, in the fullness of time, God sent Jesus. God provided a Lamb for Himself. Jesus came into the world. He was God's Final Word against sin. He was the promised, long-awaited Savior. He was the Lamb of God, and He could take away the sin of the world. The guilt that rivers of blood from animal sacrifices had been incapable of washing away, Jesus Christ would conquer and take away with a once-for-all sacrifice of Himself. From the glories and exaltation of heaven, Christ came to earth, and although, in the wisdom of God, He was the Lamb slain before the foundation of the world, yet there was a specific time on earth when God clothed Himself with the likeness of men, took on Himself the form of a servant, and came and dwelt among us. Jesus came to earth. This is how God chose to answer the question: God the Son became the Lamb of God—the Lamb of God who takes away the sin of the world.

72. A PRAISE FOR SALVATION

Gracious God, although Your wrath against sin is dreadful and fierce, thank You for pouring it upon Christ for my sake that I might be called Your child. It is a solemn thing to consider the sacrifice of Jesus for me; that You were pleased to bruise Him—to crush Your Son—to bring many sons to glory, to lead out a whole host of captives in triumphal procession. You gave Your Son as Infinite Atonement for my infinite sin against You. I am reconciled to You because of what You have done for me. That makes no human sense.

> For one will scarcely die for a righteous person—though perhaps for a good person one would dare even to die—but God shows His love for us in that while we were still sinners, Christ died for us. Since, therefore, we have now been justified by His blood, much more shall we be saved by Him from the wrath of God. For if while we were enemies we were reconciled to God by the death of His Son, much more, now that we are reconciled, shall we be saved by His life. More than that, we also rejoice in God through our Lord Jesus Christ, through Whom we have now received reconciliation.
>
> (Romans 5:7–11)

Earlier in the chapter, we are told that we have unashamed hope "because God's love has been poured into our hearts through the Holy Spirit who has been given to us" (Rom. 5:5 ESV).

Thank You for this, my God. I stand redeemed by Jesus' blood and clad in His righteousness. "Hallelujah! What a Savior!"[14]

73. CONFESSING DISCONTENTMENT

My dear Father, I am sensing a subtle discontentment with what You have chosen for these couple of days... Forgive me, and please give me grace and wisdom and yieldedness to talk this through with You now, and then confess and forsake it. I am somewhat vexed with Your choice in a couple of different realms—forgive my impudence and foolish clinging to my thoughts and ways that are decidedly inferior to Your wise, kind, and gracious will. I know that You will choose what is right and good for me and for Your other children who are involved. When I was going through the decision process yesterday, You really did lead me step by step to where I am right now, and I believe that You want me to be here and to engage in all that You are putting before me. Therefore, please, my patient and merciful God, through Your Spirit's consistent, righteous, effective ministry, turn my heart to embrace what You have chosen. I love You passionately, and I long to not grieve You by clinging to my sinful, petulant attitude. Do as You desire with me. Please be truly glorified in my life, my Lord.

Miriam K. Champlin

74. HEART EXAMINATION

CHRIST:

Do I really, genuinely, abandonedly, joyfully, uncalculatingly, purely trust Him?

Am I accurately, passionately, determinedly, hopefully, confidently, desperately, purposefully fixing my eyes on Him—seeing Him, seeking Him, desiring Him?

Is Christ my Life? Can I bear even the thought of life without Him?

Do I live only for His good pleasure and approval, or do others hold illegitimate sway in their opinions and reactions?

Am I satisfied with Christ alone? With no knowledge of the future's holdings, inability to make plans, long hours of hard work, little sleep, people's demands and expectations, my sin battles, etc.? Do I live in His promised sufficiency?

Am I thankful for all that He has chosen for me in love? Do I bless the Lord and remember all His goodness to me?

Does my life bear out the truth that Christ is enough—solely and fully?

Do I love Him like He is worthy of being loved? With heart, soul, mind, and strength?

Am I passionate—authentically, consistently passionate—about His Person, His Word, His ways, and His personal friendship with me?

Would I settle for less than waiting for Him to act? Would I be willing to manipulate things, people, or circumstances in order to bring my will to pass, rather than resting in Him and waiting patiently for His good purposes to be fulfilled?

Will I stake my life absolutely on His truth?

Do I carefully weigh the minute implications of His Word in my life and diligently apply them—with discipline, without swerving, with meticulous attention, and with loving, willing devotion?

Am I *His* in every sense of the word?

Is He satisfied as He considers my life?

Can He put His full, good pleasure upon my life, because He is the One who is Ruling in all things—sitting upon the throne of my heart?

Is He most exalted? Is the preeminence His?

Can He freely reflect Himself in me?

Is He willing and pleased to be worshipped by me, or does He find my worship unacceptable or defiled in any way?

Lord Jesus—my Lord Jesus—You know. Search me; know me; see me; lead me in the way everlasting. For Your Name's sake, teach and change me, and reveal Yourself to me and through me at any cost. I love You. I am willing, by Your grace, to trust and obey. Please receive the glory due to Your Name, because from You, through You, and to You are all things. And Yours is the glory.

Miriam K. Champlin

75. ETERNAL GOOD
IN GOD HIMSELF

The redeemed have all their objective good in God. God Himself is the great good which they are brought to the possession and enjoyment of by redemption. He is the highest good, and the sum of all that good that Christ has purchased. God is the inheritance of the saints; He is the Portion of their souls. God is their wealth and treasure, their food, their life, their dwelling place, their ornament and diadem, and their everlasting honor and glory. They have none in heaven but God; He is the great good, which the redeemed are received to at death, and which they are to rise to at the end of the world.

The Lord God, He is the light of the heavenly Jerusalem; and is the "the river of the water of life" that runs, and the tree of life that grows, "in the midst of the paradise of God." The glorious excellencies and beauty of God will be what will forever entertain the minds of the saints, and the love of God will be their everlasting feast. The redeemed will indeed enjoy other things; they will enjoy the angels, and will enjoy one another: but that which they shall enjoy in the angels, or each other, or in anything else whatsoever, that will yield them delight and happiness, will be what will be seen of God in them.[15]

76. GRATEFUL
THOUGHTS OF CHRIST

"Of Him and through Him and to Him are all things."
(Rom. 11:36)

Christ: Wisdom, Righteousness, Sanctification, and Redemption.

Christ: the Way, the Truth, the Life.

Christ: the only begotten Son of God.

Christ: the Hope of glory.

Christ: the One who will make heaven Heaven for us—without Christ, heaven itself would be utterly unsatisfying. Heaven is to be with Christ forever.

Christ: the Light of the World.

Christ: the King forever.

"Praise Him, praise Him, Jesus our blessed Redeemer."[16]

77. A MORNING PRAYER

Beautiful Savior, "Thine be the glory, Risen, Conquering Son! Endless is the victory Thou o'er Death hath won."[17] All praise to You, for You have triumphed over every enemy! You have crushed the Serpent and his hosts! You have won a most glorious victory! You lead in the triumphant procession, and we are the glad captives. We were always captives, but our former masters were harsh, destructive, and evil, and You, O Great Captain, are gentle, gracious, and good. With abounding life and joy, we pledge You our loyal, grateful service, knowing that this is merely reasonable. We ought to do nothing else, and, even at the end of a full day's obedient labor, we are still unprofitable servants. But, O my God, my Lord, my King, I pray that in me, You might find a good and faithful servant. O that my ears may hear, my eyes see, and my heart understand and do! O that in me the Lamb might receive that for which He suffered and died: a reconciled life lived to the glory of the Father. My God, I love You. I commit myself to You today. I desire to obey You, and by Your grace, I will obey You. I long for You to be pleased—that is really all that matters. Give wisdom and strength. Orchestrate the events and the people of the day. Do as You have planned, and it will be enough. You are my LORD; I have no good apart from You. Show Yourself strong.

78. CHRIST IS RISEN!

"And if Christ is not risen..." (1 Cor. 15:14) then the preaching of the Gospel and faith in Christ are futile, empty, vain, hopeless, and hollow...a miserable deception. But oh, the transformational truth: Christ is risen! God raised Him up as the first fruits of all those who will, just like their Master, be raised up in that day. Christ has risen! And this fact brings life and strength, soundness, beauty, and dynamic power to the preaching of the Gospel. Christ is risen! His work is finished; it is complete; it is eternally accomplished; there is no lack, no need for any further offering or sacrifice. Jesus paid it all. He Himself bore our sins in His own body on the tree, so that we, having died to sin, should live for righteousness. Christ is risen! And as He lives, even now, and will die no more, so will we who follow in Him. His death was once and for all, and it was sufficient. Christ is risen!

Our faith stands not in the wisdom of men but in the power of God. Our faith is rich and valid, and if we hold fast to our confidence in His faithfulness, our faith is unshakeable. The God who cannot lie has given us the light of knowing Him in the face of Jesus Christ, our risen and glorified Head. Christ is risen! This zenith of history has living, vital, daily impact. Christ is alive. He is seated at the Father's own right

Miriam K. Champlin

hand, upholding all things by the Word of His power. He has the power of indestructible life. He has innate, inexorable life. The resurrection of Christ has life-consuming implications for those who name the Name of Christ. After all, His Word says that those whom He has given life—His own kind of eternal life—should not live for themselves, but for He who died for them and rose again.

The resurrection of Christ puts every believer under eternal obligation to use the life that has been given to him in the way that the Life-Giver would have him use it. Christ is risen. And I am, too, and shall be again. The resurrection of Christ changes everything. Am I changed every day by the reality of my risen Christ and the eternal implications of His aliveness? Does the truth of the resurrection dominate my struggle with sin, my confidence in the power of the Gospel—both in salvation and in sanctification—and my growth in grace and in the knowledge of my Lord and Savior Jesus Christ? Christ is risen! And He must reign until He has put all enemies under His feet. This is yet another way in which there is no one who can compare with Christ. His resurrection sets Him apart. There is no one like Him in His Life. Christ is risen!

79. A PRAYER OF CONFESSION AND THANKSGIVING

Today, You were causing me to praise You for bringing me low. O my dear, dear Father, You are so kind to me. You know the astonishing swiftness with which I cease depending on You and stand on my own two feet (the feet You gave me, the strength You have supplied). You know how pride's presence and interminable bids for power and control dog every thought, every word, every action, every day. You know how tragically susceptible I am to pride. You know how my natural strength, both of constitution and upbringing, have hard-wired me to this, and how I sinfully boast in my own perceived riches and wisdom and strength. You see when I unmercifully tread on the hearts of others and belittle (even if only in my head) the work that You are bringing to pass in their souls, no matter how small it may seem. You see when I engage in respect of persons and fear of man. You see when I sit back and smugly survey my spiritual progress (Oh, even to confess such base sin…I find the words scorching, hideous, forgivable only by One like You, blotted out only by the immeasurable efficacy of the blood of the Lamb of God slain from the foundation of the world). You know when I rise from my knees in worshipful surrender and begin to pursue my own folly and seek my own glory. You see when lovelessness makes me harsh to others, when my impatience snaps rudely, when lack of compassion makes me willing to judge without feeling the pain of my brother keenly, in my own heart. And You are determined that my own sin will not win the day. Christ is not risen in vain! The indwelling Spirit is powerful. You have said that sin will not have dominion over me. You will not suffer me to languish in any dungeon of sin or allow any other master to command my service. You are jealous over me. And so You bring me low. You change my plans. You commandeer my time. You exhaust my physical resources. You expose my sinfulness to myself and to others. No grace but Yours is wise enough or kind enough to do this on my behalf. You bring me back to Yourself—whether running and throwing myself into Your arms or at Your feet, whether limping from the effects of a battle fought without the armor, or whether being dragged nearly against my will back to Your throne—You bring me back to Yourself. O thank You for bringing me low! Thank You for crippling me so that I might know what it is to walk in the Spirit. Thank You for fulfilling George Matheson's prayer that I have long shared: "Make me a captive, Lord, and then I shall be free; Force me to render up my sword, and I shall conqueror be. I sink in life's alarms when by myself I stand: Imprison me within Thine arms and strong shall be my hand."[18] O thank You. I praise You for slaying me so that I might learn to trust You with all my heart and not lean to my own understanding. This is infinite grace! This is steadfast love! This is longsuffering! This is like You! O thank You!

80. MASTER AND LORD

Master and Lord: we who are Yours delight to call You this. Long we served sin and self—cruel, harsh, and destructive masters. Our bondage was complete and our misery was heavy. Long we groaned under the weight of sin and self, little knowing of You and Your perfect salvation and gracious mastery. We did not know of Your plans for our good and Your eternal glory. We were lost and blind; indeed, we were dead in trespasses and sins. But You, being rich in mercy, because of Your great love—a love so great that You loved even us—made us alive together with Christ, raised us up, and made us sit together with Christ in the heavenlies. If this be not grace, what is? No one else has grace like Yours. No other is so wholly full of grace and truth as is the Savior, who came to save us and to reign in our lives. You saved us. You saved me.

Think, O my soul, of your former and your current state, and see that Christ alone has made every difference. How can you not call Him Master and Lord, for you owe Him everything?

Master, my Master, I embrace Your lordship. Control all of me. Take full command. Do whatever will most glorify You. I love You. I desire Your glory. Satisfy Yourself in my life. Make Your Name great. It is fitting for You to do all Your will. Yours is the kingdom, the power, and the glory—forever and ever.

Miriam K. Champlin

81. PSALM 2

Raging nations plot rebellion,
Peoples rise in mutiny;
Kings unite and stand defiant,
Rulers plan their treachery.
"We will not submit to Yahweh!
His Anointed we despise.
Casting off each law that binds us,
We'll do right in our own eyes."

God, enthroned in highest Heaven,
Mocks their foolish vanity,
Taunts them with profound derision,
Laughs at their futility,
Then declares in righteous anger,
"I will crush their proud domains.
I've installed My King in Zion;
On My holy mount He reigns."

Hear God's vow to the Messiah:
"Ask of Me, and I'll endow
World dominion as Your birthright:
Nations at Your feet will bow.
You, my Son, will rule with iron
All the rebel kings of earth.
Broken, like clay pots in pieces,
They'll confess Your glorious worth."

Kings of earth, receive instruction;
Rulers, heed His warning calls.
Bow to Him with joyful trembling;
Come before His fury falls.
Kiss the Son in grateful reverence,
Gladly place your trust in Him.
Blessed are the ones He pardons,
Those who own His reign within.

While meditation does not have to take hours at a time, you should try to devote quality and quantity time to it as often as possible. This reflection on Psalm 2 is the outflow of many hours spent poring over the psalm over a period of several months. Even with that, I still do not feel like I have "mastered" this text. I understand it better than I did when I began to meditate on it, and it has left its imprint on my life, but I still do not "get it" completely and I need to continue meditating on it. This poetic paraphrase of Psalm 2, then, is really an incomplete meditation, and I include it in this book to encourage you to persevere in your commitment to meditating even on complex passages that require much time and effort. Meditation is accessible to every believer, but it is not, nor should it be, easy. Knowing God is an infinite privilege—a privilege too valuable to be obtained cheaply.

Miriam K. Champlin

82. A MORNING PRAYER

Again, O my beloved Father in heaven, it is with thanksgiving that I bow to You. You are the Worthy One. You are rich toward all those who call upon You. You hear the cry of Your children. You bless with forgiveness and fellowship and strength in the inner man by Your powerful Spirit. No god except You deals in this way with his people. You are unique, set apart, hallowed in Your ways and means of dealing with Your worshippers—those who name Your Name. You have even said that You are not ashamed to be called their God and that You are preparing a city for them. Thank You for numbering me among this glorious multitude of called-out ones. I lift my voice in praise to You, in anticipation of an eternity of perfect adoration. I request, Indwelling Spirit, that You would perfect praise from my mouth and soul to the Son and the Father, because it is fitting for adoration and acclamation to accompany Your great Name. I love You, O Triune God, and worship You. You are incomprehensible yet knowable, and the way You so graciously manifest Yourself elicits the praise and adoration of my soul. Please receive honor and glory in my life all throughout today, I ask. I submit myself to You, and ask for Your ruling and overruling in all of my life. I yield my will to Yours. Temper my joys and my sorrows, my vision and my confusion as You see fit, only be pleased to be seen and known and heard by me and through me today. Spread Your kingdom and dominion in me and around me. You can do this; therefore, I leave my requests with thanksgiving before Your throne in the Name of Jesus my wonderful Savior and Elder Brother.

And one more thing: by Your Holy Spirit, arm me and enable me to use the armor rightly, so that the battle may be fought and won in Your Name and Your strength. Preserve me from leaning on the arm of the flesh, but, rather, may You win a most glorious victory. You are worthy.

83. THE JUDGE

Judge.
The Righteous Judge.
The Judge of all the earth.
Christ the Son, to whom all judgment has been committed.

One of the many portraits of Christ that spans both the Old and the New Testaments is that of Judge. As early as Genesis, Abraham addresses "the Angel of the LORD" as "the Judge of all the earth" (Gen. 18:25), and in Revelation, the Faithful and True comes to judge with righteous judgment. He sits on His throne, and He judges all men. As Creator, the right to judge is His. The primary characteristic of His judgment is righteousness. Isaiah tells us that the Spirit of the LORD will rest upon Jesse's branch and will equip Him to judge with understanding—not according to external appearances or word of mouth—and with perfect, righteous, discerning judgment. At the end of his life, Paul's testimony was that he had "fought the good fight... finished the race...kept the faith" (2 Tim. 4:7), and he was persuaded that this record would stand before "the Lord, the righteous Judge" (2 Tim. 4:8), who would give him a crown of righteousness. The minor prophets frequently use judge/courtroom imagery in their indictments against Israel. Israel was living as though they faced no final accountability, and the prophets of God definitively rebutted this attitude. Make no mistake: there is a Judge, and there will be judgment. This Judge possesses the final authority to deal with the universe as He sees fits. No one will be exempt from standing under His scrutiny, and nothing will escape His notice. Hebrews tells us that there is nothing that is not open to His sight, and that all things are laid bare before the eyes of the One to whom we will give an account. We will give account to Him, and whether we intend it to be or not, that account will be accurate. This Judge will judge from a throne. There will be no need for a jury or other legal assistants. This Judge is King, Witness, Lawgiver, Prosecutor, Advocate, Propitiation, Examiner, and Rewarder. He will see all the evidence; He will know even the motives of the heart; He will pass judgment with swift accuracy. His eyes have been described as a flame of fire. His tongue will pronounce the irrevocable sentences of eternal blessing and damnation. His execution of the sentence will be complete and consistent. He who spoke the first words will have the last word.

The Father has committed all judgment to the Son, and in the end, only that which is acceptable to Christ will matter. Christ is the Judge. When He was on earth, He admonished His disciples not to fear those who can hurt the body, but rather to fear the One who has power and authority to sentence both soul and body to hell. So, fear Christ. Reverence Him. Live for His final "well done," so that you may stand before Him as an unashamed workman. Let your manner of life speak of your awareness of your accountability to the Eternal

Judge. By your manner of life, vindicate His righteousness. He is able to save and to destroy, and He will do so with perfect righteousness, because He is Christ, the Judge of all the earth.

84. WORD-BASED INTERCESSION

PSALM 62

May their souls wait upon You, O God—the One who brings salvation.

May they find You alone to be their Rock and their Salvation and their Defense,

> and therefore may they not be shaken.

O that they would wait! Would wait wholly and solely upon You.

> Wait in quietness and hope in You.

You *are* their Rock and their Salvation and their Defense.

> May they glory in You,
>
>> rest on You.

You are the Refuge, the Hiding Place.

> May they trust in You.
>
> O that they might trust in You!

May they pour out their hearts to You, O God, their King, their Friend.

Power is Yours.

> Unwavering faithfulness and mercy and loyalty are Yours.
>
> And You are their God.

Miriam K. Champlin

Prayerfully seek to develop the habit of Biblically grounded intercession for others. Praying Scripture on behalf of others is one of the most important things you can do for them. This reflection and the next two are examples of ways you can pray through a Scripture passage in intercession. When you pray this way, you are simply opening up your Bible, walking through a text, and allowing the Word to direct your priorities and requests on behalf of others. The psalms and epistles lend themselves most readily to this type of prayer, so you may want to start there; the prophetic books and the Gospels may be profitably engaged in this way as well.

85. WORD-BASED INTERCESSION

PSALM 91

May they dwell in Your secret place, Most High God.
And abide under Your shadow…
 …finding their Refuge and Fortress in You.
 …placing their trust in Your Person.
 …accepting Your deliverance from internal fear and unrest and Your guidance in all external circumstances.
 …setting their love upon You.
May they see Your salvation and boldly say, "Yahweh is my Helper…"

86. WORD-BASED INTERCESSION

COLOSSIANS 1

May they walk worthy of You.
May they please You in all things—
    —being fruitful in every good work
    —abounding in knowing You
    —experiencing Your strengthening—yes, even
    Your strengthening them with all might,
      enabling both patience and longsuffering with joy.
May they be rich in thanksgiving to
    the Father, who has fitted them to be partakers
of an eternal inheritance,
    the Father, who delivered them from the power
    of darkness
      and translated them into the kingdom of
        His Son
          their Savior,
            Jesus Christ.
May they recognize Your magnificence and majesty, Father,
    and give You preeminence in all things.
So that the riches of Your glory may be made manifest
in their lives, and
So that others will see Christ, the Hope of glory, in
them.

87. CHRIST: THE WISDOM OF GOD

"Christ…in whom are hidden all the treasures of wisdom and knowledge." (Col. 2:3).

Among the outstanding attributes of God is wisdom. God has devoted an entire section of His Word—His revelation of Himself to us—to the subject of Wisdom. He has set a price and glory on the attainment of wisdom that is comparable to little else in God's economy. Wisdom is a glory and a crown. To possess wisdom is better than the possession of jewels and riches. Wisdom is called a tree of life to those who have it. We are told to take hold of wisdom and not to let it go. Wisdom is absolutely indispensable for life and godliness, and the wisdom of God is centered in Christ.

Christ is the Wisdom and Power of God. Christ is our Wisdom and Righteousness and Sanctification and Redemption. We are to glory in Him and in knowing Him. Even as a child, Christ was known for His increase in wisdom and in favor with God and men.

Wisdom is one of the few things that we are actually repeatedly commanded to seek, and this is noteworthy, because true wisdom is found in Christ alone. To seek wisdom—the principle thing—is to seek Christ, the Preeminent One, for that which He alone can give. So there is wisdom that may be given to us (which we are to ask for from the Father, and He will not chide us), and then there is Holy Wisdom that is marvelously unique to Christ and Him alone: wisdom that is incomprehensible to our finite minds, wisdom we will never attain, but wisdom that Christ will teach and mold us to mirror. We shall not possess holy wisdom, but we shall reflect it, just as we reflect the glory of God when we gaze steadfastly on the face of Christ. Apart from Christ, we have no hope of wisdom. But to us who believe (O the wonder of it!), Christ is the Wisdom of God and the Power of God. And we are complete—complete even in wisdom—in Him.

88. YOUR FAVOR

O my Lord, my God, my All, I give You praise. "Lord of All, to Thee we raise this our hymn of grateful praise."[19] You are worthy to receive glory and honor, riches and blessing, wisdom and strength. You are magnificent, O LORD God! You are rich in steadfast love and faithfulness. Yours are justice, judgment, wrath, and purity. Yours are righteousness, truth, beauty, and grace. Yours are humility, kindness, holiness, and majesty. Father, my Father, every perfection is Yours. You are the sole Possessor of the beauty of holiness, and yet we may earnestly and expectantly pray, "Let the favor of the Lord our God be upon us" (Ps. 90:17, ESV). So I ask for Your favor to rest on me, my King and my God. I want to be marked by You…by Your dominion, Your kingdom, Your righteousness, Your surpassing beauty. O that I might walk with You!

89. GLORYING IN JESUS

I will glory in my Redeemer who is everything, literally everything to me. I will glory in my Redeemer, who is the Keeper of my soul, and into whose hand I have committed all my being. I have nothing apart from Him, nothing kept from Him, nothing too big or too small for His care. He is the Redeemer, Jesus, the Son of God. And He became a man. He took the form of men, and being found in fashion as a man, He humbled Himself and became obedient to death, even the death of the cross. Because of this, God has greatly exalted Him and given Him the superlative Name. Every knee will bow to Him, and every tongue will acknowledge His Lordship. His Name is the superior Name—it is above every name. One of the chief wonders of His Lordship is His nearness to His people, though. He has determined to be known personally by His people. In fact, He has told them that instead of glorying in the typical human pursuits, such as wisdom, strength, riches, etc., they should glory in Him. They should glory in knowing Him and understanding Him. They should glory in opening up to Him and letting Him—in all His rich Sonship and fullness—be their own Wisdom, Righteousness, Sanctification, and Redemption. They, the beggars, should feast upon His goodness. They, the paupers, should enjoy full access to His resources.

They, the wretched, filthy outcasts, should draw near and rejoice in His love and cleansing. They, the heirs of death, should be made children of light and life. They, the estranged, should be brought near. They, the hopeless, should glory with joy unspeakable in the blessed Hope laid up for them. They should glory in Him gladly, gratefully, lovingly, richly, worshipfully, unreservedly, and exclusively, because He is who He says He is.

90. A MORNING PRAYER

God of grace and goodness, Father of unending mercies, thank You for prayer. Thank You for being the God of time and eternity. Thank You for Your sovereign providence. Thank You for Your wisdom and knowledge—there is no searching of Your understanding. This morning, I, though weak, poor, and needy, do not, and should not, hesitate to come before Your throne, for You, though almighty, rich, and transcendent, have given me an Advocate who is the recipient of Your eternal satisfaction and good pleasure. I come bearing my Advocate's righteousness and standing on the grounds of His standing with You. Having come to You through Him, let me live every moment of today under His gracious reign and authority. By the strength and grace of Your Holy Spirit, keep my heart attuned to Your heart. Let me draw near with a true heart in full assurance of faith, for You have sprinkled and cleansed my heart with the blood of Jesus, and You are faithful. Then let me, as I interact with others, have wisdom and grace to stir them up also to love and to good works. I love You and submit to You. I give You my attention—only please keep it, for I am so quickly and trivially distracted. I accept the reality of my death to sin in Jesus and my life in Him, and therefore, I yield my members in obedience and loyalty to You. Work in me continually that I might work out Your great salvation. Thank You for giving me armor with which to enter the pitched battle today. I need You and love You. I am Yours, O Lord, and I praise You for the mercy You have shown to my soul. You are a magnificent God, a wonderful Savior.

91. REVELATION 5

Then I saw in the right hand of him who was seated on the throne a scroll written within and on the back, sealed with seven seals. And I saw a strong angel proclaiming with a loud voice, 'Who is worthy to open the scroll and break its seals?" And no one in heaven or on earth or under the earth was able to open the scroll or to look into it, and I began to weep loudly because no one was found worthy to open the scroll or to look into it. And one of the elders said to me, "Weep no more; behold, the Lion of the tribe of Judah, the Root of David, has conquered, so that he can open the scroll and its seven seals."

And between the throne and the four living creatures and among the elders I saw a Lamb standing, as though it had been slain, with seven horns and with seven eyes, which are the seven spirits of God sent out into all the earth. And he went and took the scroll from the right hand of him who was seated on the throne. And when he had taken the scroll, the four living creatures and the twenty-four elders fell down before the Lamb, each holding a harp, and golden bowls full of incense, which are the prayers of the saints. And they sang a new song, saying,

> "Worthy are you to take the scroll
>
> and to open its seals,

for you were slain, and by your blood
you ransomed people for God

from every tribe and language
and people and nation,

and you have made them a kingdom and priests to our God,

and they shall reign on the earth."

Then I looked, and I heard around the throne and the living creatures and the elders the voice of many angels, numbering myriads of myriads and thousands of thousands, saying with a loud voice, "Worthy is the Lamb who was slain, to receive power and wealth and wisdom and might and honor and glory and blessing!" And I heard every creature in heaven and on earth and under the earth and in the sea, and all that is in them, saying, "To him who sits on the throne and to the Lamb be blessing and honor and glory and might forever and ever!" And the four living creatures said, "Amen!" and the elders fell down and worshiped.

(ESV)

Miriam K. Champlin

92. THE GRIEF OF GOD

An excerpt from my journal:

> "Praise Him, praise Him: Jesus our blessed
> Redeemer!"[20] You were slain and have redeemed us
> to God by Your blood out of every kindred, tongue,
> people, and nation. You have robed us in Your
> righteousness. You have made us kings and priests
> to God. You have taken sinners and made them
> saints. You have transformed enemies and made
> them sons. You have made peace through the blood
> of Your cross. You are our Peace—peace with God
> and peace with one another. You have changed sul-
> len rebels into singers of grateful praise. You have
> triumphed over sin, death, the grave, darkness, and
> the Enemy. You have manifested Your superior
> beauty as well as Your superior power, and that
> is why the ransomed *choose* to turn away from the
> offers of sin and strive to please You—because You
> are better. O for the day when ...

And at that point, I had been going to say something
along the lines of, "...every knee bows and all see and
acknowledge Your superiority—Your Lordship," but
here the Spirit began to teach me about the grief of
God over those who turn away until it is too late. Yes,
the day is coming when the Son will receive universal
acknowledgement (and that will be glorious), but some
of those who bow the knee on that day will enter eter-

nal condemnation—not the sweet sonship of those of us who have bowed the knee in this life. And the Spirit began to make me tie in many recent meditations on the love and desire and generosity of God in salvation. The Lord is not willing that any should perish (2 Peter 3:9)—He takes no pleasure in the death of the wicked (Ezekiel 33:11). He is a God gracious and merciful, slow to anger and abundant in steadfast love, and One who relents from doing harm (to those who repent) (Jonah 4:2). He is the One who, because of the great love with which He loved us—even when we were dead in sins, quickened us (Ephesians 2:4). He did not spare His own Son—that is how much He loved the world (John 3:16). So intent was He on bringing many sons to glory that He gave them a Savior at the cost of (humanly) unthinkable suffering (Hebrews 2:10). In order to bring willful, foolish, straying sheep back to Himself, He was pleased to crush His Servant (Isaiah 53:10). And so on; the teaching of the Word on this score is overwhelming: God's desire in salvation. The love of God. The immeasurable beauty of Christ. The obedient and agonizing yet joyful surrender, suffering, and death of Christ. The triumphant resurrection that began to sound the victory bell that will sound for eternity. God has shown Himself strong in salvation! He has made Himself known! He has redeemed! He has saved! He has made for Himself a great Name! He has crowned His Son, the Lion of the tribe of Judah, the Lamb, King of kings and Lord of lords forever! And by us, He will eternally display how rich His deep kindness is—the wealth of His mercy, the fullness of His love and grace. This is who He is. This is what this God is like.

Miriam K. Champlin

Therefore, when people turn away from Him—when they reject Him—when they will not have this One to reign over them—God is grieved. (Does it overcome your mind and heart to think that the Transcendent God feels pain on account of man—on account of me?) God tells us this about Himself. It was because of man's sin in Genesis 6:6 that "He was grieved in His heart." The sin of Sodom and Gomorrah was heavy/grievous. He even grieved over/became impatient with the misery of enslaved Israel—even though they were being justly punished for forsaking Him (Judges 10:16). This grief of God is perhaps one of the most surprising themes of the Old Testament: the loving, mourning, broken heart of Yahweh over the waywardness of His beloved people Israel. He expressed it in so many ways: His seemingly interminable patience (which they noticed and chose to abuse); His readiness to forgive and relent from judgment in the face of repentance (even when the repentance may not have been the caliber that it should have been: e.g. Manasseh, Ahab, the entire nation under enemy attack); and the generosity of the original covenant promises of love, peace, protection, dominion, a father-to-children relationship with them. He pursued them. He used the strongest metaphors and word pictures known to humans to convey how deeply He loved them and how horrific, how devastating their treachery was. He spoke in terms of the marriage covenant of love and loyalty, the pain that ensues when the covenant is broken, and the breathtaking love and loyalty of a faithful lover to an unfaithful spouse. He was never unfaithful to them despite the fact that they were rarely loyal to Him even for relatively short periods of time.

The rhetorical questions often voiced by the prophets are some of the most poignant expressions of His love and grief: "How can I give you up" (Hosea 11:8)? "What injustice have your fathers found in Me, that they have gone far from Me, have followed idols, and have become idolaters" (Jeremiah 2:5)? "What more could have been done to My vineyard that I have not done in it" (Isaiah 5:4)? His relationship with Israel is typical of how He deals with the children of men. It is a vivid demonstration of how much of His own heart He gives to His people—how He allows Himself to be affected by them.

Look at Calvary. Here is the apex. Here is the place that answers every question we might muster against the love of God—against His willingness to be touched by our sins, sorrows, and griefs. Here God Himself was made sin, was put to grief. O behold the Man of Sorrows! The rest of the New Testament continues to affirm this identification of God with His people. This teaching is so strong in Scripture! It is inescapable. This is the kind of love with which God loves and, therefore, the kind of grief with which He grieves.

There is no grief as deep and weighty as the grief of God. Just as He has the greatest love, so He bears the most excruciating grief. This is a sober thought, because the only reason that He is touched by grief is because He touches and is touched by us. The day is coming when God will wipe away every tear from His children's eyes, and He who bore their grief and grieved over them will remove grief from them.

The grief of God. How are we to respond to the grief of God? How can we reflect Him accurately and

Miriam K. Champlin

attractively in this facet of His character? What thanks can we give Him for His loving grief over us, for His willingness to be pained by us? My soul, worship Him and seek to know Him in His grief over souls—gaze upon the Man of Sorrows—and beholding, let the Spirit change you into His likeness to share in this part of His suffering as His child and His ambassador to those whom He desires to reconcile.

93. MAN OF SORROWS
(PART 1)

"...a Man of sorrows and acquainted with grief..." (Isa. 53:3)

Man of sorrows. Does it seem strange to you that the Son of God would bear a name such as this? Why would the One called the Lord of glory also bear a title like "Man of sorrows?" Why would the One who is eternally self-existing and self-sufficient allow Himself to be so touched by grief and pain as to be identified by His extraordinary sufferings? These are questions we must ask.

Man of sorrows. What sorrows? Whose sorrows? What does the Lord Jesus want us to learn about Himself as we meditate on Him as the Man of sorrows?

Man of sorrows. The Biblical record reveals that the grief of God is always caused by sin. Always. While this makes sense as soon as one stops to think about it, I found this to be quite sobering to my view of sin. Consider these two examples: In the days of Noah, we find that "The Lord saw that the wickedness of man was great in the earth, and that every intention of the thoughts of his heart was only evil continually...and it grieved Him to His heart" (Gen. 6:5–6, ESV). We read that when He was healing the man with the withered hand, Jesus saw the sinful, unbelieving spirits of those around Him and was "grieved by the hardness of their

Miriam K. Champlin

hearts" (Mark 3:5). In the case of Noah, the sin was blatantly obvious: violence literally filled the earth. In the case of the Jews, the sin was in the privacy of their hearts. In both cases, the sin was known to God, and He mourned over the sin and its strangle-hold on the race of men created in His image.

Man of sorrows. The unfathomable love of God is such that even when sin has utterly distorted and ravaged every part of a man, God declares that He takes "no pleasure in the death of the wicked" (Eze. 33:11). But the sin's rightful wage is death. Holy justice demands that sin be repaid in full. Holy mercy cannot righteously set aside the Divine condemnation of sinners. Yet holy love grieves. And holy love cannot give up its beloved people. Just as the love of God is unfathomable, so is the grief of God. We will never be able to sound the depths of the grief of God over sin—our sin—my sin. It is a weighty thing.

Man of sorrows. This part of the character of Christ was reflected by various men of God who saw sin as He sees it and who imaged Him in their response to sin. These men lived close to God and shared deeply in His love and burden for the souls of men. Men such as Moses, Jeremiah, Daniel, and Paul all drank many draughts from the cup of sorrow on behalf of the sin of their people. In this, they were like Christ.

Man of sorrows. But God is transcendent. He is so far above us. He is complete in His own sufficiency. He needs or lacks nothing. He ought to be untouchable (at least that is how we think). There is no logical reason that God would ever allow Himself to be touched by grief. It really makes no sense from the human perspective. Why would the Perfect One willingly be marred by what is an abomination in His sight? Why must Christ experience the terrible, crushing weight of grief over sin?

(O that I might feel an unbearable weight of grief over sin, so that I might flee from sin rather than tolerating, excusing, or even embracing it!)

Two comments:

1. *Pausing for prayer before intentional meditation is necessary. We are weak; we need the Spirit's illumination. It is always appropriate and needful to seek Divine assistance from the Author of the Word, the One who delights in making Himself known. For example, "Father, this is a name of Christ that I have never meditated on before. I need Your enablement. Dear Teacher of truth and Revealer of Christ, please guide my thoughts in the Word, so that I may know and worship my Jesus more rightly." This is what I did when, after reading Isaiah 53, the Spirit began to draw my heart to meditate on "Man of sorrows."*

2. *This meditation (like the "Wonderful" meditations [16]) makes use of repetition as a key tool. Part of meditation is repetition. It is going back to a thought, a Scripture, a truth over and over and over. Instead of primarily using the name as the starting point for a lengthy discussion (e.g., the "King" [66] and "Judge" [83] meditations), go back to the initial thought frequently and examine it from a different angle. The method is different, but the net result is similar.*

94. MAN OF SORROWS (PART 2)

Man of sorrows. Read Isaiah's Servant Songs. They paint such a glorious picture of the Servant of the LORD. Here is One who does the work of God rightly, loyally, wisely, continually. Here is One who images Yahweh perfectly, and He is described in magnificent ways and in terms of the Spirit that rests upon Him. Read about Him. Admire Him. Be fascinated by the descriptions of Him that are found in His Word. Long to know Him. And then find that He became the Man of sorrows, and it was because of sin. Yes, because of your sin. Because you, like a sheep, went astray. Because you turned to your own way. Because you sinned, because you were at enmity with the God who loved you, God required the wages of your iniquity in the death of His Son—this righteous, matchless Servant of the LORD. And Christ, God Himself, took upon Himself the punishment of sin. He became the Man of sorrows.

Man of sorrows. There is no grief like the grief He bore. He bore our grief and carried our sorrows, and all the while, we still despised Him. We mocked Him and thought that He was a victim of God's judgment— that He was being "smitten of God" (Isa. 53:4, ESV). The truth is that "He was wounded for our transgressions; He was crushed for our iniquities; upon Him was the chastisement that brought us peace, and with His stripes we are healed" (Isa. 53:5, ESV). He who knew no sin was made sin for us, so that we who knew no righteousness could be made the righteousness of God in Him. He, who alone had the right to perfect intimacy and continual communion with the Father, was forsaken by God in order to provide sinners with an imputed righteousness, a cleansed heart, and a way of access through which they could draw near to God.

Man of sorrows. Christ atoned for our sins at a dreadful cost. But this is how matchless and worthy Christ is (just try to let this sink in): even in the midst of the agony of sin-bearing, the Bible tells us that Christ, for the joy that was set before Him, endured the cross, despising the shame. Christ's love was so deep and His obedience to the Father so strong that even on the cross, forsaken by God, He kept His mind fixed on the joy of bringing many sons to glory and declaring their names to His Father. This is Christ, the Man of sorrows, the Mighty Conqueror, the Redeemer, the Glorious King, the Lamb of God who took away the sin of the world. This is why God has so highly exalted Him and given Him the Name that is above every name. This is why Christ is Lord.

To go along with these meditations, you may want to read the "Servant Songs"—Messianic passages throughout the latter part of Isaiah.

Isaiah 42:1–9; 49:1–12; 50:4–9; 52:13–53:12; 61:1–3

Miriam K. Champlin

95. A PRAYER OF ADORATION

"More love to Thee, O Christ! More love to Thee!...This is my earnest plea..."[21] My Father, my own Father... yet how can one title express even a fraction of You, of Your relationship with Your own, of Your greatness and goodness? Yet You have chosen human speech, human terms, human communication...You have always condescended to us like this. You have always talked to us in ways that we could access (if not fully grasp). And then, as Your ultimate proof of Your determination to identify with us so that we can be identified with You, God became flesh. Such humility! I am seeing Your humility in a way that I have never seen it before! The humility of Christ was a reflection of Your humility, dear Father. In His meekness and lowliness of heart, He was manifesting You to us. You have always acted in gracious humility toward Your people, and truly, Jesus the Son exegeted You perfectly on this point (as on every other). He displayed humility like we have never seen before, and thus we, who have not seen God at any time, have had You declared to us by the Son. We have seen You. The Son in the Father, the Father in the Son! And oh, the glory of it! The wonder of it! There is no other god like this. None. You are separate! You are holy! You are the One True God. O thank You!

96. A PRAYER IN BATTLE

You will surely win the victory. O my Lord, my soul and body are faint, but You will uphold me—of this I am confident. Thank You. I dare not fear; I need not fear. You, O Lord, are a Shield for me, my Glory, and the Lifter-Up of my head. You are my Rock, my Song, my Strength, my Salvation. You are my Hope, O Lord Jesus—thank You for taking pleasure in those who hope in Your mercy. By Your grace, I will obey You. I choose to seek first Your kingdom and Your righteousness. I stand in the armor You have provided—the belt of Truth, the breastplate of Righteousness, the helmet of Salvation, the shoes of Gospel-readiness, the shield of the Faith, the Sword of the Spirit, and prayer. Captain, the battle is Yours, and I am grateful. You must fight for me. I love You and need You. And, my Light, my Love, be glorified.

Miriam K. Champlin

97. HIS GRACE

You've got to think of His grace until you can't help
be like Him.[22]

–Tim Keller

98. KNOWING GOD

Job 21:14 says of the wicked, "...they say to God, 'Depart from us, for we do not desire the knowledge of Your ways." Just reading those words sends cold dread into my heart. Who could utter such words in the face of the Almighty? Although I often stray by reason of my own willfulness, my love of my self, and my lack of love for my God, yet, in the core of my being I desire the knowledge of God more than anything else, and I am destitute and miserable when not walking with Him in intimate communion. Who can say to God, "Depart from us, for we do not desire the knowledge of Your ways"? Yet this is what the heart of the wicked is like. Does it not stand to reason that the heart of the righteous should be the complete opposite: "Please come to us, for we earnestly desire the knowledge of Your ways"? Psalm 10:4 declares, "The wicked in his proud countenance does not seek God; God is in none of his thoughts." It should be said of the righteous, "The righteous, in humility of heart, always seeks God; God is in all his thoughts."

The knowledge of God, thoughts of God, desire for God ought to be the believer's perpetual preoccupation. What else is there? Is there another pursuit worth giving your mind, thoughts, talents, skills, and passions to? That is why Paul said, "This one thing I do" (Phil.

Miriam K. Champlin

3:13). The Lord told Martha, "One thing is necessary" (Lk. 10:42). David cried out, "One thing I have desired of the LORD," (Ps. 27:8). To the rich young ruler who had everything else, Christ said, "One thing you lack," (Mk. 10:21), and the lack of that "one thing" canceled every other asset he possessed. The Bible speaks of the necessity of having a single eye (Lk. 11:34), of serving in singleness of heart as to Christ (Col. 3:22), of loving the Lord our God with all (Mk. 12:30). "All your heart" is a repeated theme in the context of knowing and walking with God. Caleb and Joshua were commended because they wholly followed the Lord (Num. 32:12). Are we able to say with the psalmist, "With my whole heart I seek you" (Ps. 119:10, ESV)? When "the eyes of the Lord run to and fro in all the earth," does He find that my "heart is loyal to Him" (2 Chron. 16:9)? Ah, let us not, let me not, be sidetracked from diligently pursing the knowledge of God.

PRAYERFUL APPLICATION

O God, my God, keep me from destroying my soul in this manner. May I never, never harden my heart and mutter, as I skulk off into my own ways, "Depart from [me]; for [I] do not desire the knowledge of Your ways." Rather, teach me to fear You, keep Your commandments, obey Your voice, serve You, and cling to You (Deut. 13:4).

99. INCOMPARABLE

Thank You for Your sovereign, gracious wisdom. You are a kind Master. Your rule is good; it is benevolent; You are the King, and such a King. There is no earthly comparison to You as King. Even the best of Israel's kings or a good historical king—these still had so many glaring, destructive faults and short-sightednesses. But not You, O Wisdom and Strength; not You, Fairest Lord Jesus. You are the Eternal King, and all Your ways are just, righteous, true, worthy, perfect, good, and glorious.

Miriam K. Champlin

100. A MORNING PRAYER

O my Lord, my open, empty hands I raise to You, in worship, in gratitude, and in supplication. "Lord, I am willing to receive what You give, to lack what You withhold, to relinquish what You take, to suffer what You inflict, to be what You require."[23] Oh, that You would come and fulfill all Your purposes for Your glory in me. You are worthy of honor, glory, blessing, riches, praise, and dominion. Because You are the Creator, You have supreme rights. It is right for Your Son to have the pre-eminence. It is wrong for created beings to seek their own glory, and yet we do. We do with tireless diligence. Yet You have not destroyed us and created a new race of those who would give You the glory due to Your Name. Rather, You chose to redeem—to make it possible for slaves of sinful self to become slaves of righteousness and holiness. You redeemed through the sacrifice of Christ, once for all. Now You have given Him the superlative Name and have commanded all men everywhere to repent. Thank You for this Good News—a Gospel for the nations! Oh, may Your kingdom come!

So teach me to live out my kingdom citizenship while I sojourn here. Teach me to number my days and gain a heart of wisdom. Enable me to represent You accurately and attractively. I give myself wholly into Your keeping, Faithful Creator. Let my self be put to death, so that the life of Jesus might be made manifest in my mortal body. He is so fair, the Altogether Lovely One—may He be seen and made much of. May I submit to His lordship. I need the Holy Spirit's work to empower me for what You have called me to do, so please keep my ears tender and open to His sweet voice. Let me not harden my heart, but find in me, I pray, a heart of steadfast love and faithfulness to You, my King and my God.

I love You. I love You. Let obedience be the proof of my love. Thank You for armor that equips me on every front for the battle against sin. Captain, lead on. Your sure victory gives me the hope and strength I need. And so I put my trust in You and my hand in Yours. Bring glory to Yourself.

101. DIVINE AUTHOR

At Mount Sinai, God wrote His words on tablets of stone and gave them to the people by the hand of Moses. Then, still using Moses, God breathed out the Pentateuch. These first five books of Divine Authorship, forming the foundation for the whole of Scripture, are fascinating, intricate, literary masterpieces. From the elaborate structure and ironies of Genesis, to the breathtaking Exodus narratives, to the holiness code of Leviticus, to the gracious heart of Deuteronomy, the variety of style, content, literary devices, thematic emphases, and intended application reveals the mind of Him who is perfect in wisdom. Ponder the Lord as the Eternal Author.

Author.

Divine Author.

God, the God of the Word … the Written Word of God.

Just as God created spoken language and used it from the beginning to reach into the lives of people to make Himself known, so He has also been using the written word to communicate His Person, His ways, His Commandments, and His glory for millennia. God has authored words—written words—eternal words.

Scripture is the fullness of God's written words to us. This divinely breathed-out Book is truth, eternally enduring Truth, and God means for us to reckon with it in every part of our lives. It is sacred and profound in and of itself, and within its contents, we find numerous examples of God's written messages and the varying responses of the human recipients of the messages.

God cut a covenant with the nation of Israel, but they disregarded it. Even though God plainly wrote His requirements, Israel had no room in their hearts for the writing of God's Law, because their sin was engraved upon their hearts. They had other writing to which they adhered, and thus, they lightly esteemed the Word of God. A grievous exchange!

After the initial giving of the law, God continued to write words for His people. He gave them recorders to reflect His perspective on their history. He gave them psalmists to lead them in right worship. He gave them wise men to capture in sayings and proverbs the essence of a life lived in the fear of the LORD. He gave them prophets to write and to proclaim oracles. The children of Israel had a God who was near them—who literally tabernacled with them. His words were near them—even in their mouths and in their hearts. These people had the words of God written on their doorposts and led lives that outwardly conformed, in most ways, to the mandates of the law, but their stony hearts were lawless, refusing to be internally shaped and dominated by the words of Yahweh. This internal rejection was manifested in the actions of the people—perhaps most graphically when Jehoiachin literally cut up and burned the scroll containing Jeremiah's message from the Lord (Jeremiah 36).

But Yahweh is rich in mercy. His mercy is inexhaustible. He saw the condition of their hearts and had mercy on them. He determined to give them new hearts, and He gave words to Jeremiah to record His intent. Jeremiah wrote of a time when Yahweh would take away the people's sin-engraved hearts of stone and give them hearts of flesh. Upon these new hearts, God would write His Laws—for the first time, the law would be inscribed internally, and their conformity would not be merely external. The Word of God, written on their hearts, would lead them in truth and righteousness. This writing of the Law would actually effect real, eternally valuable change. God would author His new covenant by sending the Word into the world, and as people believed on the Living Word, God gave them power to become the sons of God and wrote His Law on their hearts.

In New Testament times, God continued to use human instruments to record His words in writing. As God breathed out His words, He preserved them for the generations to come in the form of writing. The Divine Author manifested His profound wisdom in the Canon, and the New Testament writings form a magnificent tapestry of revelation that spans different genres, different target audiences, different human authors, and different functions. God's Book displays His marvelous providence by its sequential arrangement—not chronologically or by human instrument, but providentially designed for a magnificent progressive revelation of Truth.

God's Book, like Himself, is eternal—it will endure forever: something that no human writing can claim. This Word is a living and powerful communication. There is an almost literal sense to words "leaping off the page" and coming into one's heart and mind to reprove, rebuke, correct, instruct, strengthen, command, and enable. In so many, many ways, the Word of God mirrors the mind of God to us. O how the beauty and glory of God are manifested in His Words! He wrote His words so that we might read them and know Him and treasure Him thousands of years later. He gave us His Word, and in His Word, Himself. Every author invests some degree of himself in what he writes, but God vested His Writing with His own infinity of wisdom, love, grace, power, truth, faithfulness, holiness, and richness. God is the Ultimate Author, and as such is to be heard, read, studied, loved, obeyed, and worshipped.

In the temporal sense, writing will be one of God's final acts in His historic work of redemption, sanctification, and glorification. Revelation 22 tells us that the servants of God will enter His city and will worship Him. We will see His face, and *His Name will be on our foreheads* (Revelation 22:4). Think of it! God will write His Name on our foreheads—the mark of absolute and eternal domination. We will be *His*—finally, completely, consummately, eternally, practically, irrevocably—*His*. That which was begun at salvation will be perfected. What for years has been true of us positionally will then be full reality. There will be no inconsistencies and no more warring of the two inner laws. He will write His Name on our foreheads! How fitting it is that He, who for so long has had His peoples' names engraved on the palms of His hands, will, with those infinitely glorious and precious hands, reach out to engrave His Name on us! Time will pass away, and "Eternity will be too short to comprehend His grace,

Miriam K. Champlin

Not long enough to tire of the radiance of His face."[24]
Time will pass away and with it, all that pertains to
time, but the Word of God will endure eternally. The
Word of God is settled in heaven. Not one letter or pen
stroke thereof shall be lost. God the Author has established His Book, and it will stand forever.

God is the Eternal Author.
He has authority, wisdom, and power.
His Book is like Him—it is holy.
There is no other Book like it.
It reveals its Author—its Holy Author.
The Written Word leads to the Living Word.
Believe and bow the knee.

102. ALLEGIANCE
TO CHRIST

My God, my Father, it is fitting for Your Name to be set on high. It is good and right for You to receive everlasting glory. It is a joyful thing for You to be made known and boldly proclaimed. Thank You for shining in our hearts, so that we might give the knowledge of the glory of God in the face of Jesus. Thank You for Jesus—Savior, Master, Redeemer, King, Advocate. I worship You, Mighty Trinity. I extol Your virtues. I admire Your beauty. I praise Your grace. I adore You. And, dear, dear Father, I seek You—not primarily Your gifts and pleasures, but You. I yearn to know You. Be my Vision exclusively. Let no other promised joys allure my soul; give my eyes discretion and discernment to see through all the false offers of life, hope, and joy, and to cling to You alone for that which You alone can provide. O my Lord, I need and love You unspeakably much. I swear my allegiance to You and own You alone as my Master and Lord.

103. THE CORNERSTONE

In Zion laid
By God alone,
The Sure Foundation:
Cornerstone.

God's Church is built
On Him alone.
Unshakeable:
This Cornerstone.

And growing thus
By Him alone,
The Church reflects
Her Cornerstone.

True unity
In Him alone:
All praise to Christ:
The Cornerstone!

Believers, stand
On Him alone!
The Solid Rock:
Our Cornerstone.

And living thus
For Him alone,
We magnify
Our Cornerstone.

The many: one
Through Him alone,
To worship our
Chief Cornerstone.

Elect of God,
He is alone
Both Lord and Christ:
The Cornerstone.

Miriam K. Champlin

104. A PRAYER OF DEPENDENCE

I was working on the task You cut out for me this evening, but I just realized that I was basically doing it by myself. O my Lord, my Friend, my Love, my Teacher, my Illuminator, my Joy, my God, my Life, I do not want to work without You. I long for Your presence and companionship and enablement. Please come and infuse these minutes and hours with Your own sweet fellowship and lordship. Come and rule. Come and fill. Come and quicken. Come and make glad. Come and enlighten. Come and do what only You can do. I love You and gladly yield to You and Your mastery. Open my mind. Take me within the veil. Do not let me harden my heart. I want to hear Your voice. I want to think Your thoughts. I want to see Your truth. I want to live out Your good pleasure. I want to love You rightly. I want You to be preeminent. I want to demonstrate my gratitude for Your rich, sweet love to me. Thank You for loving me.

A SAMPLE MEDITATION
PROCESS

PSALM 90

As I was slowly reading Psalm 90 one day over lunch, I realized that I was not at all following the train of thought or the spirit of the passage, so I started at the beginning again, this time consciously engaging the text. I got lost again. So I skimmed to the end, and started again. Same thing. I started asking the Lord to teach me, to open my eyes and my mind to what He was seeking to communicate in this passage. I then repeated the cycle several more times, each time with the same result. I was not getting it. This probably sounds familiar to most people. So then what? Well, time was up, and I had to move on to other things. Tomorrow, I will go on and read Psalm 91, right? That is definitely the temptation, but it is rarely the right response. If you realize you are not understanding something, the Lord has drawn your attention to it for a reason, and He intends to teach you, if you will let Him. So go back to it. The next day over lunch, I went back to Psalm 90. More of the same, but this time, I pinpointed where I was losing the thought connections—verse 3 and verse 12. And as I kept reading, I was encouraged to notice that that was where I should have lost the thought connections: those are the places where the thought flow changes. But I still did not understand it at all. I did not see how or why the changes took place, or where they were going, let alone what I was supposed to understand from it all. And then time was up. This happened several days, and over the course of those days, I began reading Psalm 90 as often as I got a chance.

"As I was slowly reading Psalm 90 one day..." Note the word "slowly." In this case, it is synonymous with "thoughtfully," and it is extremely important. You have to start with this. Speed-reading the Word will have little effect on you. You must prepare your heart and be willing to slow down and engage your mind and your spirit. It is presumptuous to think that God is going to send you a lightning-strike epiphany every time you thumb through a few chapters or verses.

When I run into a text like this, I often find it helpful to copy and paste the text into a blank document. I take out the verse numbers and try to think of the entire passage more holistically, and then I go through and create a layout of the text that displays the relationships between sentences and phrases. So that is what I did—or started doing:

Psalm 90

Lord, you have been our dwelling place in all generations.
    Before the mountains were brought forth,
        or ever you had formed the earth and the world,
from everlasting to everlasting you are God.

You return man to dust
and say, "Return, O children of man!"
> For a thousand years in your sight are but as yesterday
> when it is past,

> > > or as a watch in the night.
> You sweep them away as with a flood;
> they are like a dream,
> > like grass that is renewed in the morning:
> > > in the morning it flourishes and is renewed;
> > > in the evening it fades and withers.
> For we are brought to an end by your anger;
> > > by your wrath we are dismayed.

You have set our iniquities before you,
> our secret sins in the light of your presence.

For all our days pass away under your wrath;
we bring our years to an end like a sigh.
The years of our life are seventy,
or even by reason of strength eighty;
yet their span is but toil and trouble;
they are soon gone, and we fly away.
11 Who considers the power of your anger,
and your wrath according to the fear of you?
12 So teach us to number our days
that we may get a heart of wisdom.
13 Return, O Lord! How long?
Have pity on your servants!
14 Satisfy us in the morning with your steadfast love,
that we may rejoice and be glad all our days.
15 Make us glad for as many days as you have afflicted us,
and for as many years as we have seen evil.
16 Let your work be shown to your servants,
and your glorious power to their children.
17 Let the favor of the Lord our God be upon us,
and establish the work of our hands upon us;
yes, establish the work of our hands!

(ESV)

I got started, but ran out of time. We all operate under time constraints. Meditation—even on difficult truths or passages—is not solely dependent on your having hours at a time to devote to it. The next time that I got back to it, I continued until I had to stop, and so on, until the layout of the text looked like this:

Psalm 90

Lord, you have been our dwelling place in all generations.
    Before the mountains were brought forth,
      or ever you had formed the earth and the world,
from everlasting to everlasting you are God.

You return man to dust
and say, "Return, O children of man!"
    For a thousand years in your sight are but as yesterday
      when it is past,
                    or as a watch in the night.
     You sweep them away as with a flood;
     they are like a dream,
       like grass that is renewed in the morning:
          in the morning it flourishes and is renewed;
          in the evening it fades and withers.
    For we are brought to an end by your anger;
           by your wrath we are dismayed.
You have set our iniquities before you,
       our secret sins in the light of your presence.
    For all our days pass away under your wrath;
    we bring our years to an end like a sigh.
     The years of our life are seventy,
     or even by reason of strength eighty;
     yet their span is but toil and trouble;
     they are soon gone, and we fly away.
Who considers the power of your anger,
     and your wrath according to the fear of you?

        Miriam K. Champlin

So teach us to number our days
  that we may get a heart of wisdom.
Return, O Lord! How long?
Have pity on your servants!
Satisfy us in the morning with your steadfast love,
  that we may rejoice and be glad all our days.
Make us glad for as many days as you have afflicted us,
    and for as many years as we have seen evil.
Let your work be shown to your servants,
  and your glorious power to their children.
Let the favor of the Lord our God be upon us,
  and establish the work of our hands upon us;
  yes, establish the work of our hands!

Your purpose in doing a layout of the text is to get a feel for the structure and thought flow of the passage. You are going to note the main clauses, indent the subordinate clauses, under them, line up parallel ideas, display any lists in the text, and generally try to track the progression of the passage. Doing a display of the text like this compels the meditator to deal with every phrase and think through how it relates to its immediate context and to the whole. It provides a level of objective perspective and more intimate familiarity with the text itself as the text is considered phrase-by-phrase or even word-by-word. The layout does not have to be strictly grammatical, but you should pay attention to the grammar if possible. (For example, in verse 14, "Satisfy us in the morning with your steadfast love" is the main clause and makes the main request, and "that we may rejoice and be glad all our days" is a subordinating clause that gives the reason for the request, so it is indented underneath it.) Often, attention to the grammar and syntax will help you tap into the writer's train of thought. Be prayerful and reflective as you work through doing a text display.

By the time I reached this stage, I had been meditating on Psalm 90 for a couple of weeks. The next
time that I had opportunity to sit down and work on
it, I began to fill in some thoughts around the text, but
it took a couple more weeks and a several more writing sessions to completely process and record what the
Lord had been teaching me. In the meantime, the text
had been shaping me. Meditation had, by the grace of
God and enablement of the Spirit, worked understanding, delight, and transformation in my heart.

PSALM 90

A Prayer of Moses, the man of God.

This prayer was offered by Moses during the forty years
of wilderness wandering. Israel was living in the very
presence of a God who tabernacled with them and led
them day and night with cloud and fire. Israel was also
literally experiencing the trouble, futility, and death
expressed in verses 3–11. It is helpful to consider the
original context from which this prayer arose. Think
of the Exodus, the travel to the border of the Promised
Land, the rebellion, the turning away, the wrath of God,
the sentence for their sin, the years in the wilderness,
the battle for survival in the midst of barrenness, the
constant struggle of faith, the daily reminder of sin and
punishment, the continual death, and the weariness of
perpetual sojourning. Then think about the promises,
the Tabernacle, the presence of God in their midst, the
future hope of the Promised Land, and the abundant
evidence of God's care and provision, even in their
present condition. Put yourself (as much as possible) in

these circumstances, and may the Lord allow your heart to begin to understand and join in this prayer.

> *Lord, you have been our dwelling place in all generations.*
> *Before the mountains were brought forth,*
> *or ever you had formed the earth and the world,*
> *from everlasting to everlasting you are God.*

These opening verses wed God's eternal vastness and transcendence to His presence and fellowship with His people. The Everlasting God is the Dwelling Place of His people. The Creator of time and space is the trans-generational habitation of His own. An itinerant people—whether moving across land or through life—finds in God a permanent residence, an eternal habitation. How beautiful! Truth about God is always beautiful: sometimes terrifying, but even then it has a terrible beauty that cultivates a proper fear of God.

Take a moment to consciously examine and list the character of God as revealed in these verses. Two explicitly mentioned names of God: Lord and God. A couple of roles: Creator and Dwelling Place/Refuge. Attributes: personal/knowable, eternal, powerful, creative, not bound by time, transcendent, supreme, stable, changeless, and enduring. These are all either explicitly mentioned or clearly implicit, yet unless you stop to meditate, to read with love and attention, you will go right through these verses without ever pausing to adore the God they reveal.

In verse 3, however, we face a striking contrast.

You return man to dust
and say, "Return, O children of man!"
> *For a thousand years in your sight are but as yesterday when*
> *it is past,*
>> *or as a watch in the night.*
> *You sweep them away as with a flood;*
> *they are like a dream,*
>> *like grass that is renewed in the morning:*
>>> *in the morning it flourishes and is renewed;*
>>> *in the evening it fades and withers.*
> *For we are brought to an end by your anger;*
>> *by your wrath we are dismayed.*
You have set our iniquities before you,
> *our secret sins in the light of your presence.*
For all our days pass away under your wrath;
we bring our years to an end like a sigh.
> *The years of our life are seventy,*
> *or even by reason of strength eighty;*
> *yet their span is but toil and trouble;*
> *they are soon gone, and we fly away.*
Who considers the power of your anger,
> *and your wrath according to the fear of you?*

How does this follow from verses 1–2? God destroying
His people? Why the wrath and the death? Suddenly,
instead of eternal immutability, we are presented with
jarring transience and futility. What changed? The
object in focus. The first two verses are focused on
God. The next eight verses focus on God's dealings
with man. Man is in view (through the lens of God's
judgment), and the contrast is painful. God is eternal. Man is not. God is strong. Man is fragile. God
is holy. Man is sinful. God is free. Man is subject to

time and trouble. God is angry. Man is destroyed by God's wrath. Man's bondage to transience is compared to a dream, to grass, and to a sigh. This is man's lot. This is man's experience. This is what the wandering Israelites saw on a daily basis, as they died one by one under the wrath and punishment of God, as their days were literally eaten up by the toil and trouble they had incurred by their own sin and rebellion. And this is the reality that faces us. The picture is dark and disturbing. Readers might be tempted, as the Israelites were, to question the truth of verses 1–2. Is God really for us? Is He truly our Refuge? Will He remain, even after death and destruction have ravaged our lives? Will His anger burn forever? What is the connection between these concepts? Are they mutually exclusive? How should man respond to the companion truths about God and himself? What response is God seeking?

> *So teach us to number our days*
> *that we may get a heart of wisdom.*
> *Return, O Lord! How long?*
> *Have pity on your servants!*
> *Satisfy us in the morning with your steadfast love,*
> *that we may rejoice and be glad all our days.*
> *Make us glad for as many days as you have afflicted us,*
> *and for as many years as we have seen evil.*
> *Let your work be shown to your servants,*
> *and your glorious power to their children.*
> *Let the favor of the Lord our God be upon us,*
> *and establish the work of our hands upon us;*
> *yes, establish the work of our hands!*

When confronted with the truth about God and the truth about ourselves, we must respond with humble teachability. Thus, the final portion of this psalm is devoted to asking the Lord to reverse the flow of our lives toward folly and futility, to have mercy in the midst of judgment. We need God Himself to teach us. We pray to the Everlasting God, our Dwelling Place, asking Him to bless our short, sinful lives by displaying His works and glorious power. We beg Him, in His kindness, to give lasting significance to the work of our hands. We are who we are. We are finite. We are sinful. But we were formed to dwell with the Eternal—in the Eternal—and we yearn for our lives to bear the stamp of His permanence, and even more: His presence and favor. We offer our prayer to the Eternal God, because we believe that He is a God of pity and steadfast love and that He will indeed manifest Himself in blessing, just as He has in wrath. We who have seen the power of God's wrath now request the favor of seeing His glorious power revealed to the generations that will follow us. We have learned that our satisfaction and gladness are sourced in Him. If the Lord will be on our side, if He will have pity on us, if He will satisfy our hearts, if He will restore gladness to us, then we have hope. If *He* makes us joyful, it will be real joy. If *He* teaches us to live wisely, even our brief lives will be worthwhile. We must respond to truth with humility and prayer.

Centuries after Moses wrote this psalm, Micah of Moresheth, another man of God, brought a message from God to wrath-cursed rebels. He also ended his proclamation of truth with a prayer—a prayer with remarkable thematic similarity to Psalm 90. After prophesying much judgment, Micah bursts out in praise of God's saving steadfast love.

But as for me, I will look to the LORD; I will wait for the God of my salvation; my God will hear me. Rejoice not over me, O my enemy; when I fall, I shall rise; when I sit in darkness, the LORD will be a light to me. I will bear the indignation of the LORD because I have sinned against him, until he pleads my cause…Who is a God like you, pardoning iniquity and passing over transgression for the remnant of his inheritance? He does not retain his anger forever, because he delights in steadfast love. He will again have compassion on us; he will tread our iniquities underfoot. You will cast all our sins into the depths of the sea. You will show faithfulness to Jacob and steadfast love to Abraham, as you have sworn to our fathers from the days of old.

Micah 7:8–9, 18–20, ESV

This is what God is like. The truth about your sin is a dreadful reality—a reality you can neither escape nor bear. It is too hard. You cannot bear it, unless…unless the Everlasting God is your Dwelling Place and the God of your salvation. If He is, live in Him and rejoice.

It is my hope and prayer that, having walked through a sample meditation process on a passage, you will be encouraged to believe that meditation is a feasible task: you can do it. The written part is only reflective of the thought process and is merely a helpful step. Throughout the weeks of scattered writing on Psalm 90 were many days of having it running through my head, praying over it, reading it whenever possible, and regularly asking the Spirit to teach me about it. There is an intricate partnership between the Lord's kindness and grace in reminding you to meditate/His setting your thoughts on the Word and your conscious choosing to meditate and discipline your thoughts to return to the truth. You cannot meditate on the Word by yourself, yet neither can you dismiss your part in exercising yourself to godliness. God has given you commands and responsibilities in this realm—commands with rich rewards for those who obey, so be obedient and be blessed. Meditate on God's Word as you go through your days.

Reducing your meditation to writing is not essential, but I do highly recommend that you keep a record/a prayer and meditation journal. Writing develops a level of invaluable discipline and precision in your thoughts about God, your worship of God, and your prayers to God. You may choose to use a notebook, a daily index card, or (like me) your computer as your recording means. Regardless of your choice, find a system that works for you, and use it to the glory of God to further your growth in knowing Him.

Miriam K. Champlin

HOW TO READ
YOUR BIBLE

When you read the Word, read it to know God. Every time you open your Bible, your primary interest should be to know and understand God and glory in Him. Always be asking, "What does this tell me about God?" "Where is God in this passage?" "What is God communicating about Himself through this account?"

As you read the Bible and as you go through your day, you ought to be on the lookout for God. God gave us the Bible to teach us about Himself, and the entirety of Scripture is profitable to that end. God also sovereignly rules your life and intends to manifest Himself to you day by day so that You can know Him better. It is of paramount importance that you hear and read the Word and that you live in light of what God intends you to learn, so you need to develop an eye for seeing, admiring, and scrutinizing the Person and work of the Trinity. Here are some ideas to help you develop this kind of God-awareness as you read the Word and go throughout your day.

1. Look for verses that contain multiple names of God, and keep a list of them. This sounds simple. It is. But it is very valuable. By doing this, you create an accessible pile of names and char-

acteristics of God that you can refer to whenever the need arises.

A brief sampling:

> But Abram said to the king of Sodom, "I have raised my hand to *the LORD, God Most High, the Possessor of heaven and earth*, (Gen. 14:22)

> But I am poor and needy; yet *the LORD* thinks upon me. You are *my help* and *my deliverer*; do not delay, *O my God*. (Ps. 40:17)

> Thus says *the LORD, the King of Israel*, and *his Redeemer, the LORD of hosts*: "I am *the First* and I am *the Last*; besides Me there is no God. (Isa. 44:6)

> Thus says *the LORD who made it, the LORD who formed it to establish it* (*the LORD is* His name): (Jer. 33:2)

2. Find a specific thought about God that occurs throughout Scripture and make note of it. E.g. God is unique.

> "Who is like You, O Lord, among the gods? Who is like You, glorious in holiness, fearful in praises, doing wonders? (Ex. 15:11)

> O Lord, there is none like You, nor is there any God besides You, according to all that we have heard with our ears. (1 Chron. 17:20)

> Among the gods there is none like You, O Lord; nor are there any works like Your works. (Ps. 86:8)

3. Be aware of books or passages that emphasize a particular name or attribute of God (e.g. Job: "The Almighty," Isaiah's "Servant" songs.)

4. Key into themes that accompany knowing God such as "seeking," "preparing the heart," "the fear of the Lord," "one thing," "diligently," etc.

5. Look for God's works all around you every day. The Bible teaches that Creation (Job 36–41; Ps. 8; 19; Prov. 6:6–8; Isa. 40) and the works of God (1 Sam. 12:24; Ps. 77:12; 143:5; Luke 2:19) are to be sources for meditation. Ask the Lord to teach you about Himself through your daily life. After all, He is the One who has sovereignly, wisely, and kindly ordained your circumstances, so He must be planning to use them for your good and His glory.

6. Highlight a couple of attributes for "chronic meditation." What is that? Often the Lord takes us through a period of time where He clearly emphasizes a certain facet of His character. Through intense struggle and growth, He teaches us to prize that particular part of His nature. But then we move on to other spheres. There is nothing wrong with that necessarily (being finite, it is impossible for us to remember everything at once). It is profitable, however, to allow the Lord to make a few of His perfections personally dear to you, and to keep those constantly circulating, or at least immediately accessible. This means that you are always on the alert for new ways to see and appreciate those perfections, fresh ways to think of and talk about

them, and accurate ways to display them. Simply attaching an appropriate adjective to bring out an element of an attribute, and then keeping that little phrase in the forefront of your mind for several hours or several days will work thanksgiving, worship, and transformation in your heart. How does this work? Let's consider an example: grace. Think about God's grace for a moment. How often do you think about it? Are you truly grateful for it, or do you take it for granted? How would you describe it? What are some superlatives you could attach to it? How can you give thanks for it? In what ways can you reflect it? Is the thought of God's grace still fresh and sweet to you? Meditate on grace. Let your mind linger over these phrases: "the triumphant adequacy of His grace,"[25] "the infinite efficacy of His grace," "invincible grace," "the dynamism of His grace," "relentless grace," and "rich grace." Tuck some of these thoughts away where you can access them readily, and refer to them often. Admire the grace of God. Do not ever let it become old to you. Make His grace a lifelong topic of frequent meditation and praise.

7. Meditating with a friend. Here is an idea that can be practiced by one person, but is often sweetest when shared with a likeminded friend (or friends): Alternate back and forth with attributes of God—one person says an attribute and the other responds with a Scripture verse or phrase that pertains to that attribute, and then lists another attribute. Variations on this theme are delightful: recalling names and titles of the Trinity back and forth; rehearsing "I am" state-

ments vs. "but God" statements; choosing one theme and quoting verses or singing songs on that one topic, and so on.

Explanation of "I am, but God" statements: one person cites something that is true about himself and his sinful condition, the other responds with a truth about God that pertains to His sufficiency or triumph in that very struggle. "I was blind, and even now, I tend to walk in sin and darkness." "But God commanded His light to shine out of darkness, and through the work of the Spirit, He has made you see. And now, as you behold the face of Christ, you are being transformed into His image from glory to glory."

8. Reading in large segments. People usually read the Bible a chapter or two at a time. While this not necessarily "bad," it should be regularly supplemented by reading large portions together in one sitting. Remember, getting the big picture is vital. You cannot understand the individual pieces accurately unless you know how they are functioning in the grand scheme of things. The Old Testament narratives are continuous stories with no original chapter breaks within the books. Read them like that. Try reading the whole book of Joshua or Judges in one sitting.

You may not be able to do that with a book as large as Kings or Chronicles, but even with the longer books, try to break it into just two or three readings. You will miss a lot of little details, but it will help orient you to the big picture. The New Testament epistles are letters, written to be read in one sitting (though certainly also to be re-read and studied). There is immense value in reading the treatise to the Hebrews from start to finish without interruption. After you have read and gotten a feel for the overall picture of what God is saying or doing in a book, then you can go back and engage the smaller portions of the book with increased profit. It would be difficult to overstate the importance of this method of Bible reading. You do not read any other book a few isolated paragraphs at a time, and you should not read the Bible *only* that way. You need the big picture. Use this tool!

9. Overlapping chapters. This suggestion ties in with the previous one. Even when you are reading a chapter or two at a time, make sure to overlap them. Do not just read them once and move on the next time you read. Your goal is to understand how it all works together, so you have to read it together. You can do something like read chapters 1–2, then 2–3, then 1–3, then 3–4, then 2 and 4, then 1–3, then 4–5, then 1 and 5, etc., so that you are tracing, doubling back, and re-tracing the thoughts, themes, arguments, and word pictures of the text. This is especially important for the prophets and the epistles, but it also holds value for the narratives and wisdom literature as well. In reading and understanding the Bible,

Miriam K. Champlin

there is an inseparable connection between the parts and whole, and you cannot afford to ignore either the scope of the whole or the impact of the parts.

10. Feel free to write in your Bible and your other devotional books. I do not like to do a lot of writing in my books, but I do use a pencil to make selective marks and comments in the text of my books. If, however, you find that prolific marking, color-coding, etc, helps you, then take some time to devise a system that works for you, and start implementing it. There are plenty of color-coding and note-making systems available. You can look some of them up online, select one, and adapt and adopt it, or you can just start from scratch. Whatever you decide, be sure your method works for you: i.e. a system that you can remember, that you can use consistently, and that is accessible to you wherever you go and whenever you are reading or writing.

CONCLUSION

> If I have observed anything by experience, it is this:
> a man may take the measure of his growth and
> decay in grace according to his thoughts and medi-
> tations upon the person of Christ and the glory of
> Christ's kingdom and of His love. [26]

Prayer and meditation on the Word are the two most
foundational elements of a relationship with God, the
two things that we are exhorted to do without ceasing.
Meditation and prayer are God's designated means for
growth in relationship with Him. To meditate on God
is to know God, and to know God is to worship Him.
God is a personal God, and it is the joy and substance
of life to know Him and be known by Him (Galatians
4:9). Paul describes it as "the surpassing worth of knowing Christ Jesus" (Philippians 3:8, ESV). If you want to
know God, meditation is a non-negotiable. You cannot
know God without this. You cannot come to God your
own way; you have to come to Him through His Word
and through the person of His Son. As we come to
God through Christ, we engage in warm, living fellowship with the creating, saving God. Nothing impacts a
person like authentic friendship with God. Fellowship
with God is transformational to one's life. So cultivate
your walk with God! Seek Him. Love Him. Spend

time with Him. Pursue Him. Listen to Him. Think about Him. Obey Him. Know Him.

Knowing God is not easy, but it is worth it. The daily implications of having a personal relationship with God are excruciating and exhausting. But nothing can compare with the richness and fullness of life that comes from walking in intimate communion with the One who is Light and Life.

In Matthew 11 (please look it up and read it), Jesus addressed a crowd of religious people who claimed that they wanted to know God, while they were actually rejecting the One whom God had sent to them. In vv. 25–26, Jesus prays and thanks the Father for concealing Himself from those who boast in their own wisdom and understanding and for revealing Himself to the humble and lowly. He then turns back to the crowd and states, "All things have been delivered to Me by My Father, and no one knows the Son except the Father. Nor does anyone know the Father except the Son, and the one to whom the Son wills to reveal Him. Come to Me, all you who labor and are heavy laden, and I will give you rest. Take My yoke upon you and learn from Me, for I am gentle and lowly in heart, and you will find rest for your souls" (vv. 27–29). In other words, Jesus tells them that in order to know the Father and in order to know peace and rest, they have to come and learn of Him. The truth of Jesus' statement still stands and so does His invitation to come, to know Him, to know the Father through Him, and to find rest in Him.

So by the Spirit, come to God through Jesus, learn of Him, meditate on Him, obey Him, and find rest for your soul. Come and know God.

ENDNOTES

1 Trans. Edward Caswell in Formby's *Catholic Hymns*, "May Jesus Christ be Praised"
2 Charles Wesley, "Arise, My Soul, Arise"
3 Charles Wesley, "O For a Thousand Tongues to Sing"
4 Charles Wesley, "Hark! The Herald Angels Sing"
5 Samuel J. Stone, "The Church's One Foundation"
6 Edward Mote, "The Solid Rock"
7 Stanza 1—Isaiah 57:15; Stanza 2—Philippians 2; Stanza 3—2 Corinthians 3. Stanza 4 references "salvation's mystery," which is related to 1 Peter 1's description of salvation as something the angel's desire to look into; it calls the believer the "temple" of God, which links to 1 Corinthians 6; and it requests the Triune God to "make Your home within my soul," which reflects Paul's prayer in Ephesians 3 that "Christ would dwell in your hearts"—that He would be at home in their hearts.
8 Last line amended by me for accuracy's sake.
9 Isaac Watts, "When I Survey the Wondrous Cross"
10 John W. Peterson, "O Glorious Love"
11 Joe Tyrpak, "I Plead for Grace." Copyright 2009 *churchworksmedia.com*. Used by permission.

12 Unknown

13 Francis Scott Key, "Lord, with Glowing Heart I'd Praise Thee"

14 Philip P. Bliss, "Hallelujah! What a Savior!"

15 Jonathan Edwards, "God Glorified in the Work of Redemption," in The Sermons of Jonathan Edwards: A Reader, ed. Wilson H. Kimnach, et al (1999): pg. 74–75

16 Fanny J. Crosby

17 Edmund Budry, "Thine Be the Glory"

18 George Mattheson, "Make Me a Captive, Lord"

19 Folliot S. Pierpoint, "For the Beauty of the Earth"

20 Fanny Crosby, "Praise Him! Praise Him!"

21 Elizabeth P. Prentiss, "More Love to Thee"

22 Of First Importance. "Think about His Grace." Message to the author. 1 Mar. 2009. Web.

23 Author Unknown

24 Avril Fries, "Looking at His Face"

25 These phrases are mostly transcribed from the prayers of Dr. Douglas MacLachlan, a former professor of mine, whose evident gratitude for and fascination with the glorious grace of God drew my heart to meditate on and savor the grace of God.

26 John Owen, The Works of John Owen, Vol. 9, pg. 475

-

Lightning Source UK Ltd.
Milton Keynes UK
UKOW02f1354180816

280976UK00001B/115/P